MAGNETIZED

MAGNETIZED

Conversations with a
Serial Killer

CARLOS BUSQUED

Translated from the Spanish by
Samuel Rutter

CATAPULT
NEW YORK

ISBN: 978-1-948226-68-4

Jacket design by Jenny Carrow
Book design by Wah-Ming Chang

Catapult titles are distributed to the trade by Publishers Group West
Phone: 866-400-5351

Library of Congress Control Number: 2019949692

Printed in the United States of America
10 9 8 7 6 5 4 3 2 1

The following text is the condensed result of over ninety hours of dialogue with Ricardo Melogno, recorded between November 2014 and December 2015. The conversations were much longer and more disparate, and the topics were covered with less continuity and greater chaos than in the current text. My edits respect the words of the interviewee while compressing, grouping, and organizing them chronologically and thematically, with the goal of providing structure to his story. I believe I have respected the concepts expounded by Ricardo, but I take full responsibility for any differences or mistakes arising from the editing process.

This text was authorized by the Juzgado de Ejecución Penal No. 1 in Morón, Buenos Aires Province.

Buenos Aires
September 2016

A current that circulates via a conductor generates a magnetic field around the conductor. The intensity of the magnetic field is proportional to the current circulating.

Ampère's Circuital Law

MAGNETIZED

1

<u>I was told that someone saw you levitate.</u>

[*Melogno furrows his brow, then smiles with amusement.*]
Who?

<u>Someone who knew you from Unit 20 and was con-</u>
<u>victed again. They brought him here, and when he saw you,</u>
<u>he asked to be kept as far away as possible. He said that you</u>
<u>were evil, and that he had seen you levitate.</u>

Oh, I know who that is, haha . . . Well, you see, that
kid's real impressionable. Among other major issues he has.

Here's the thing with me. In prison, things pass from
mouth to mouth and they start adding up. Over the years
it's sort of snowballed. Even now, when they send in the
search parties—they're not guards from here, but from
the "regular" prison, and they come every two or three
months—they find the shrine in my cell with all the offerings and the candles, they say: "Old man, what are you

getting up to here? What's all this strange stuff?" But these guys are more modern nowadays, they ask more out of curiosity, not out of fear.

[*On his left arm he has a tattoo with three symbols stacked above one another: at the top is a 666, in the middle an inverted crucifix, and on the bottom a reversed swastika. The line of symbols is flanked by two snakes writhing rampantly from left to right.*]

<u>Why the reversed swastika?</u>

The regular swastika, the one used by the Nazis, represents turning toward the sun, toward the light. So I got mine tattooed like this, turning toward the darkness.

<u>Who gave you this tattoo?</u>

I did it myself, watching my arm in a mirror.

<u>Why do you pray to the Devil?</u>

Because I feel him.

<u>Doesn't the Devil inspire evil deeds?</u>

If that's what I thought, I'd be a Christian. Evil comes from within a person, not from religion. Just because someone has a dark side . . . that doesn't necessarily mean they're evil in their life. The idea that because I worship Satan, I must be a son of a bitch, is a Christian idea. It's like saying that the youth has turned to shit because they listen to rock and roll. Youth turns to shit for a thousand other reasons, but not because of rock and roll.

Youth Turned to Shit

In September 1982, a series of brief, strange, and almost restrained murders took place in the city of Buenos Aires. Over the course of one week, in an area spanning no more than a few blocks in the neighborhood of Mataderos, the lifeless bodies of four taxi drivers were found. Each corpse appeared in the early hours of the morning, slumped forward in the front seat of a taxi, with a .22 caliber bullet hole in the right temple. The taxis were parked on dark corners, with their interior lights and engines switched off and their headlights ablaze. There was no sign of robbery, although registration documents for the vehicles and ID for the victims were missing. Except for the last incident, the taxi meters all read zero.

Only three of the four murders made the news. On September 24, the *La Razón*, *Crónica*, *La Prensa*, and *Clarín* newspapers devoted only a few lines to the discovery of the body of "A.R." on the corner of Pola and Basualdo Streets. Four days later, slightly more space was dedicated to the discovery of "C.C." on the 1800 block of Oliden Street. The individual in question was not yet dead, but he was dying. He had a hole in his skull that was bleeding profusely, and in the end, he died on the way to the hospital. Following this second incident, the 42nd Precinct organized a sweeping operation, swarming Mataderos with their own officers as well as reinforcements from the Robbery and Assault, Crime Prevention, and Investigations units. Despite all this activity, on September 28, the body of "J.G." was found on the corner of Basualdo and Tapalqué Streets, only four hundred meters from the other bodies. Later, two more attempted holdups of taxis would take place in the same area, in which the drivers received wounds from blunt objects but emerged relatively unscathed. One of the drivers gave a description of his attacker, which was drawn up into an Identikit and disseminated through the newspapers and television.

Police were unable to shed light on the crimes. The only facts ascertained by the agents were that all of the crimes were the work of a single individual and that the perpetrator had not moved from the rear seat of the taxi during the attacks.

The gaps in the investigation were filled in by the Buenos Aires media with hypotheses of varying degrees of craziness.

"We cannot rule out the possibility that this psychopath is a woman in disguise, with very short hair."

"The murderer might be a student attending night

school who is mentally unstable and attacks taxi drivers after class."

"This maniac called the 42nd Precinct and vowed to attack again, saying that nobody could stop him."

"The murderer is a psychopath with a complex personality; it is thought that he kills only on the corners of streets whose names have an even number of letters in them."

Taxi drivers began attacking passengers they thought resembled the Identikit. In several sweeps, the police detained over twenty "persons of interest," none of whom turned out to have anything to do with the crimes.

On the morning of October 15, 1982, a man presented himself at the Palace of Tribunals in the Federal Capital and asked to speak with the judge presiding over the case. He said he was coming to "clear his name." The taxi murderer was his brother, who at that very moment was with their father, having breakfast in an apartment in Caballito. He offered to take the police there. He assured the judge that his brother was unarmed and that they would be able to arrest him without incident.

The mysterious murderer turned out to be twenty years old, and he looked completely different from the Identikit. His name was Ricardo Luis Melogno.

During the judicial interrogation, the young man admitted to the three murders, but denied having committed the last two attacks without fatalities. The surviving taxi drivers did not identify him as the culprit.

He confessed to another murder in Lomas del Mirador, close to Mataderos but on the other side of General Paz Avenue, outside the city limits of Buenos Aires. When the police from the Province of Buenos Aires were consulted, they confirmed that a taxi driver, with a surname of T——, had recently been found murdered in identical conditions to the previous three. In fact, the three Mataderos killings weren't previous but subsequent murders. Chronologically, the fourth crime was actually the first.

Otro Taxista Asesinado en Mataderos

UN taxista fue asesinado en la madrugada de ayer en el barrio de Mataderos. El grave suceso se conoció recién esta mañana en esferas policiales, que guardaban absoluto hermetismo en torno al sangriento episodio. De cualquier forma, pudo saberse que la víctima fue ident-

ficada como Carlos Cannet de 35 años y que el crimen fue perpetrado a balazos fue cometido en la calle Olcieri al 1900, a dos cuadras de los predios del mataderos. Algunos tras-sendidos indican que el chofer, que conducía un automóvil Fiat 125, murió al ser trasladado en grave estado

al hospital Santojanni. Este es el segundo caso en pocas hora en que un taxista es asesinado en dicha zona, pues se recuerda dias atras fue muerte a tiros en la calle ... 1500 — a pocas cuadras de otro nuevo hecho — el de otro taxista que con aun siglas sin aclarar

Detienen a 4 Sujetos que Habian Ultrajado a una Niña de 11 Años	Se Investiga el Robo de 3.000 Millones de Pesos en una Joyeria	**HORRIBLE** Condenan a reclusión perpetua a una mujer que dio muerte a sus dos hijas	Maniobras con Recetas Falsas, Investigan en Farmacias de La Plata

Asaltan y asesinan a otro taxista

Efectivos de la Seccional 42º del barrio de Mataderos hallaron en estado de agonía a un taxista que momentos antes recibió un disparo en la cabeza tras ser asaltado. La víctima agonizó antes de ingresar al hospital en el que se produjo su deceso.

Otro chófer de taxímetros fue herido en un asalto en el barrio de Mataderos

Mataderos: conmoción e intensa búsqueda por los ataques a chóferes de taxímetros

Buscan al Psicópata que Asesinó a los Tres Taxistas, a Balazos, en Mataderos

CONTINUA la investigación por parte del personal de la División Homicidios y la comisaría 42º en procura de aclarar las circustancias de tres taxistas en el barrio de Mataderos. Cabe destacar

Realizan Intensas Batidas Para Hallar al Autor de la Muerte de Tres Taxistas

CONTINUAN en forma activa los operativos que realiza la Policía Federal para hallar al

ASESINATOS DE TAXISTAS

Detienen a 17 sospechosos

Continúan los procedimientos por asesinatos de chóferes

Los Crímenes de los Taxistas

Se Hallaría Detenido el Asesino de los Taxistas

Estaría detenido el autor de los asesinatos de los tres taxistas, ocurridos a fines del mes pasado en Mataderos. El acusado de los homicidios habría sido objeto de un minucioso examen psiquiátrico por parte *determinado que su personalidad sería la de un paranoico. Todos los crímenes tuvieron una similitud, ya que los taxistas fueron ultimados a balazos en la cabeza, a escasas cuadras de distancia.*

...ayó el Asesino de los Taxistas, un Desequilibrado Mental Denunciado a la Policía por el Propio Hermano

Fue detenido el autor de los asesinatos de taxistas

Enfermizo... rencor a los taxistas

REVELACIONES SOBRE... MULTIPLE HOMICIDA

No se mostró arrepentido el asesino de los taxistas

Nuevos detalles de la detención del acusado de atacar a chóferes

Iniciaron los Médicos Forenses el Examen Psiquiátrico del Asesino de los Taxistas

El juez de instrucción doctor Miguel Ángel Camiñas prosigue las diligencias tendien...

Pídese examen médico para Ricardo Melogno

El Asesino de Taxistas

Tres taxistas muertos. Dos a punto de ser asesinados. Un mismo barrio (Mataderos) y un arma de un mismo calibre (22). Los dos chóferes sobrevivientes no reconocen en el único detenido, Ricardo Luis Melogno, entregado por su propio hermano, al hombre que los atacó. No hay fotos que permitan comparar el identikit. No hay datos precisos. Sólo interrogantes.

"Tengo un problema adentro", manifestó Melogno a un vecino el miércoles

Vecinos de Melogno nos manifestaron en forma coincidente que se trataba en... haber sido desertor andaba en cuestiones un tanto extrañas como drogas y brujería... ubicados en el techo de la vivienda del asesino.

A Problem Inside

Apparently, the suspect's father was the first to find evidence, when he discovered the victims' identity documents, which his son guarded jealously. While many minor details remain unknown, it's clear that the anguished father asked for advice from his other son, and together they arrived at the conclusion that they should deliver Ricardo Luis to justice.

In the paternal home, a .22 caliber pistol was found, presumably used in the commission of the crimes.

Ricardo Luis Melogno was interrogated for six hours, during which time he readily confessed to the crimes and was examined by forensic doctors. Throughout the investigation he was observed to be calm, without ever showing signs of nerves. When he was asked why he committed the crimes, he refused to answer.

Neighbors in the area agreed upon a

description of the young man as timid and withdrawn, clearly concealing a horrifying tangle of feelings and impulses beneath a calm exterior. They also said that Ricardo sometimes left the house in his military service uniform. By that time he had been discharged from the military, after extra time was added to his service as punishment for having lost or stolen weapons of war on the grounds of the Villa Martelli Army Barracks, located on Avenida General Paz, between Tejar and Constituyentes Streets.

His father was well regarded in the neighborhood, and concerning his mother, it was said that she lived at a different residence, apparently in a shantytown.

One neighbor, who did not wish to give his name, said that on occasion he had come across Ricardo acting strangely, doing things like standing still in one place, lost in his thoughts, his eyes fixed to the ground.

Clarín, October 17, 1982

According to statements gathered, he is a strange young man, with obvious psychological problems. He was described as very shy and withdrawn, with few links to his neighbors, whom he mostly ignored, along with other

young people of his own age. "He's very tac-
iturn, not the type to strike up conversation."
For the last few months he had been living in a
room at the back of his father's house, detached
from the main building.

His strange personality moved the mag-
istrate assigned to the case to call for psychiatric and psychological examinations to be
undertaken in the coming hours to determine
if Melogno's mental characteristics are normal.

La Razón, October 18, 1982

Throughout the interrogation Melogno re-
sponded in detail to questions asked by the
judge, but he remained consistently mute
whenever he was asked why he had committed
the crimes. He never stole a dime. So what was
the motive for the chilling executions? Silence
was the only answer.

There seem to be few concrete facts about
his life. No one knows where to find his father
or brother. It is as if the ground has swallowed
them up. No relatives have come forward,
nor anyone who can provide a photograph of
Ricardo Luis Melogno. Where is the mother?
That remains unknown. Just one more unan-
swered question to add to the many others that

have prevented us from reconstructing the life of a murderer who is barely twenty years old.

Revista Gente,
the week after the arrest

Without admitting to friendship or regular contact, a neighbor indicated that he regularly spoke with Melogno, and that he didn't seem like an unbalanced individual. "The only time I saw him looking strange was last Wednesday, when we passed each other on the street. When I saw the desperate look on his face, I asked him what was wrong. He said 'I have a problem inside.' But I have no idea what he meant by the word 'inside.'"

La Prensa, October 18, 1982

"He's Not the Sort of Person Who Loses His Cool and Kills a Man."

[*Doctor Miguel Ángel Caminos, who arrested Melogno in 1982 and took his first statement.*]

The rhythm of my work life means that I find people guilty or I find them innocent, and then I forget about them entirely. If you asked me what sentences I handed down last week, I couldn't tell you. But there are some cases that have an impact on you, and you remember them. Back then [in 1982] I was still a court investigator. There was a lot of uproar around this case because every day, or practically every day, another dead body turned up in Mataderos. The police had cordoned off the neighborhood, it was a huge operation, but they hadn't come up with anything.

Then one day Melogno's brother showed up with two lawyers and told us that his father had found the taxi drivers' documents, and that he didn't know what to do about it. He said to come over to his place, that his brother was there. He was with his lawyers—he wanted to clear his name and wash his hands of the whole thing.

<u>Do you have any memories of the family? Could you tell
me something about the father, for example?</u>

Hmmm . . . no, not really. I have stronger memories of
the brother.

<u>What impression did you have of him?</u>

I had a good feeling about him. He was worried about
his brother, because he'd found the documents and the
other things. He seemed overwhelmed. I promised him
that if his brother was the culprit, I'd look after him, and
that I wouldn't leave him in the hands of the police. The
police were pretty brutal in those days, they used a lot of
illegal methods.

I hurried out of the courthouse and went into the office
at the Third Precinct. I told them I was a court investigator
and that they should put a squad together and come with
me. I'd explain everything on the way.

We arrived at the building, and I went up with my sec-
retary, the forensic examiner, and the police captain. I was
first out of the elevator and when I went into the apartment, Melogno was just standing there in the living room.
He didn't look like a brutal murderer, just a regular, skinny
kid. There was nothing impressive about him at all. I introduced myself and asked how he was feeling. "I don't know,"
he said. "I don't know what's happening to me," is what he
said, or something like that.

I put him in the squad car and we went back to the
courthouse, where I took his statement in my office with

the forensic examiner. Melogno told us that he would wait until a voice told him "that one." He let the taxis go by until he heard a voice that told him "that one."

In the interrogation did he say that he heard "a voice"?

Um . . . something indicated "that one" to him. He could sense it, but he didn't know how or why. He couldn't say why he killed them, or how he chose them.

He spoke at length, and I had the impression that he was trying to get it all off his chest. I remember he told me that he kept the identification documents of his victims, that he wasn't interested in their money. When I asked him what he did with the money, he said he spent it at a restaurant in Mataderos. I asked him why he kept the documents, if they were some kind of trophy. His answer was "something like that." I think I drew that answer out of him. As I recall, I asked him something along the lines of "Why do you keep the documents? Are they trophies?" And he said yes. It wasn't something he said spontaneously.

He didn't seem crazy. He wasn't talking nonsense, he wasn't raving. This may have confused the forensic examiner. He insisted that Melogno wasn't crazy, that he could be charged because he was responsible for his actions and was making things up. He categorically stated that Melogno was not crazy. That didn't seem the case to me—in fact it was quite the opposite. Because this was just . . . killing for the sake of killing. There was no reason for it. People always kill for a reason, and then later they lie to avoid taking responsibility. Here there was no motive. It was killing for the sake of killing, plain and simple.

In the newspapers it was reported that when he was asked for the motive behind his killings, Melogno remained silent and refused to make a statement.

He didn't know why. I remember that very clearly.

Did he say he didn't know why? Or did he refuse to make a statement about why he killed? The distinction is very important.

I don't remember the finer details. I am sure, however, that he didn't refuse to give an answer. I was left with the impression that he was somehow relieved, that a weight had been lifted from him after all this.

Did he become emotional at all during the statement?

No, not at all. He didn't even try to pretend. I don't recall him ever saying he regretted his actions. He didn't conjecture either, or try to curry favor. In my job you hear remorse all the time, but mostly it's the "I'm sorry, please reduce my sentence" type of remorse. In general remorse comes across as rather speculative, but with Melogno there was none of that. It was more like relief.

What was his mood like during the interrogation?

He was very serious [*pauses to reflect*]. Yes. Very serious. The great mystery here is why he chose those particular taxi drivers. Because there's no logic to it. When I asked him about it, he said it was "very complicated."

I think this was one aspect of Melogno, not his whole personality.

Once I had a terrible case. It was a family of eight siblings. They were good, hardworking people, a very close family. One of the siblings was the accused. This guy moved out of the family home, and after a while started dating a girl, who he decided to introduce to the family. One day, he and his girlfriend and one of his brothers met up in a bar, and they sat down together to have a Coke. They were sitting at the bar and the waiter brought them a large bottle, and then the brother served the girlfriend before serving himself. The first brother didn't like this, and asked himself, "Who does he think he is, pouring Coke for my girlfriend?" And then when they left the bar and were standing out on the street, the brother by chance happened to be between the guy and his girlfriend. From then on, the guy began to weave a web of jealousy, to seethe within. This guy lived in a boardinghouse where he shared a room with another man, and the web of jealousy took the imagined form of the brother and the roommate having orgies with his girlfriend. He threw this in his girlfriend's face, and the girlfriend told him he was crazy, but there was no way to convince him. One day, the guy took a leather-cutting knife and decided he was going to have it out with her once and for all. "I'll bring it up with her," he thought, "and if she defends my brother, I'll kill her." He went over to his girlfriend's house, and as soon as he started talking about his brother, the girlfriend interrupted, yelling, "Can you let this go already?" or something like that. That's when the boyfriend pulled out the knife and slit her throat. It was a deep, horrible cut that sliced through her vocal cords, but by some miracle he didn't kill her. That man was later declared free of mental illness by psychiatrists. He was absolutely crazy, but the thing is, his actions had a clear relationship to the situation. If you spoke to the guy about anything else at all he was a normal, reasonable person. But if you brought up the brother and the girlfriend he would start frothing at the mouth.

So what I'm trying to say is, this could have been the case with Melogno: he might be absolutely fine, except when it came to . . . There's something that made him choose taxi drivers. It's a strange choice, but a deliberate and repeated one. At the same time there's no explaining it.

But something, there has to be something.

There's no motive. It's not like he got angry with the taxi drivers then killed them. He was no murderer [*reflects, then laughs*]. "He was no murderer . . ." Yes, of course, he *was* a murderer: he killed four people. But what I mean is, he had no temper. He wasn't the kind of person who loses his cool and kills a man, or who gets angry with his wife and sets fire to her.

Thirty-Four Years in the Life of Ricardo Melogno, According to the State

October 1982. Report from the Federal Capital. Melogno makes no statement, but agrees to be interrogated. His responses are precise and seemingly honest. He didn't take just any taxi that came along. He waited until something inside him indicated that the next taxi to pass would be "the one." Some kind of order from inside. Not a voice, but a feeling coming from the body. During the journey, he gave the victim no indication of what was to come, nor did he make threats. He felt that in this way the victim would suffer less. He says he felt like he was watching a movie; like he was just an observer. He remembers the four murders in fragments. He does not remember the exact moment of shooting, nor the deaths of any of the four victims. In each case, after firing the weapon, he took the driver's documents, switched off the engine, and stayed inside the cab for a moment. He took the documents because of the photos, as a means of self-defense. By taking the photos, the spirits of the dead would never bother him. He was not interested in the money.

"When I got out of the car, I walked away and thought: 'How strange that I feel nothing.'"

Melogno completed primary school, repeating the third grade. He made it to the second year of high school. He spent the period preceding his arrest in a situation of homelessness. The family had split and they were violent with each other. He did not keep bad company. He had a case pending for concealing a crime from the military authorities, for which he had been incarcerated for nine months at the 601st Battalion's facilities in Villa Martelli in Buenos Aires. Due to his incarceration, he was not deployed in the Malvinas conflict.

Appearance: Shows disinterest in everything around him. Facial expressions neutral, except for a mocking smile.

Attitude: No sign of mental activity. Indifference to the immediate environment.

Demeanor: Neatly dressed, freshly bathed, and hair kempt. Wearing worn shoes. When this is mentioned by the interviewers, he says he will ask for new ones.

Attention: Slight disturbances in both forms (spontaneous and voluntary). It is as if his application is imperfect or inadequate to reality.

Memory: Intact.

Allopsychic and Autopsychic Orientation: Globally in time and space, awareness of his situation but not of his illness.

Ideation: Distorted.

Association of Ideas: Normal. Content of ideas sometimes absurd.

Judgment: Deviating from normal logic towards the deranged.

Thought: Certain delay in process. Incapable of argumentation.

Imagination: Deranged.

Emotional Functioning: Quantitative disturbances. He is indifferent, showing no emotional nuances at all. He says that he is not in prison, he is "in his own world."

Psychological Evaluation: More than dialogue, engages in monologues at times. Seeks shelter in a fantasy world. Particular and practical intelligence, difficulties with abstract and complex thought. Difficulty evaluating human situations. Gives up when required to engage in sustained mental activity.

Conclusions: Schizophrenia combined with psychopathic personality. At the time of the murders, Melogno could not understand the criminality of his actions.

1984. General examination in Buenos Aires Province. Marked egocentrism. Frozen affect. Normal cognitive functions, without sensory-perceptive or thought alterations. Immature, although of normal intelligence. Well-adjusted to reality. When asked about the value he attaches to life, he says he cannot answer as he has never given it thought, and his own life is worth nothing.

Presents as distant, indifferent, without emotional attach-
ment. Always withdrawn. Conclusion: anomalous personality. Psychopath with schizoid, perverted, and hysterical
traits. Not a mental illness, but a diversion from normal
personality.

1985. Declared unfit for trial by means of insanity for the
three murders committed in the Federal Capital. The court
trying him for the murder committed in the Province of
Buenos Aires considers him responsible for his actions. He
is sentenced to life in prison. In the psychiatric report, there
is a lack of consensus on the psychiatric cause of his illness.
Manifestations of chronic delirium, compatible with paraphrenia or paranoia. Intervention from two jurisdictions
(Federal Capital and Province of Buenos Aires), but cases
are kept separate. In one jurisdiction, he is deemed insane,
and in the other he is criminally responsible. Transferred
to the Devoto prison.

1987. Transferred to Unit 20 of the Borda Hospital.

1995. By letter, Melogno seeks the full details of his charges
and asks to be given the name of his defense attorney. Some
spelling mistakes in the letter, but otherwise correctly
written. He continues to write letters: in 1997 he asks once
again to see his attorney.

2000. Psychiatric report indicates that he may have suffered a psychotic break at the time of the crimes. He appears to have recovered. Tendency toward magical thinking. Antisocial personality disorder with schizoid nuclei. Tendency toward isolation. Use of activities to give meaning to his life: works in the unit's laundry, and in a workshop where household electrical items are repaired. Also learns and practices vellum crafts.

2002. Report shows no new developments. It is reiterated that the prison framework and clear rules function as a "container" for Melogno.

2003. New note in which Melogno states that for over ten years he has received no sanctions.

2003–2005. Improvement in his social habits, but still a preference for solitude. Work helps him keep things together. He describes emotional or interpersonal experiences in a matter-of-fact or abstract way. Pays most attention to the objective and formal aspects of social or emotional events.

2005. Diagnosis: schizoid disorder. It is determined that without having gained any insight on the crimes, Melogno is still considered dangerous, leading to a recommendation that security measures remain in place. Expert reports always unfavorable.

2006. MMPI-2 test. Melogno recognizes various psychological problems, with openness and readiness to discuss them and capacity for self-criticism. Displays mental resources for self-defense. Able to control hostility. Self-involved attitude. Cautious, with possible ritual activity. Superstitious. Tendency toward introspection, with a preference for solitude. Introverted, unsure, indecisive. Obsessive thoughts (brooding). Low tolerance for tedium, wide range of interests. Work efficiency, goal-setting, enterprising attitude. Regarding treatment, instead of garnering insight, tends to rationalize and resists interpretations.

In November 2006, a new expert determines that due to the presence of a schizoid disorder, Melogno remains dangerous, and that, in general, he responds poorly to treatment. He is not deranged.

2007–2008. Harsher report, but with the same diagnosis.

2009. Diagnosed with serious psychopathy, ongoing detention advised to facilitate further therapeutic work, as Melogno is still dangerous.

2010. Report from the Unit 20 treatment team. Melogno has adapted well and undertakes maintenance work.

Always ready to undertake interviews with experts. They describe him as a solitary person and note that his meetings with his father somehow opened up the world of social relations. Has projects for the outside but doesn't believe he will be released. His psychiatric issues are under control, according to reports. Not undertaking pharmacological treatment. Diagnosis: schizoid personality disorder. Does not fall under the criteria for ongoing penal institutionalization, and should continue treatment in a public hospital, without need for confinement. Melogno seeks release and transfer to a public hospital.

Confusion between sentences and jurisdictions. The defense attorney seeks parole. Experts from the Supreme Court (psychiatrists and psychologists) determine the following: serious schizoid personality disorder. From a psychiatric standpoint, Melogno remains dangerous. He should remain confined where he is.

July 2011. Unit 20 is disbanded, and Melogno is transferred to a facility run by the Inter-Ministerial Mental Health Program in the Ezeiza Penitentiary Complex.

September 2015—Present. Melogno's whole sentence has been served. However, he remains incarcerated. As a mentally ill individual, he is under the purview of a civil court, which determines that the best course of action is that he remain in jail. This creates a legal conflict, given that the civil judge violates the law by demanding that Melogno remain incarcerated without a sentence. Negotiations with public hospitals and private psychiatric institutions, who are reluctant to take on his case.

2

Some professionals believe that ever since I was a child, there has been something wrong with me. I always played alone, and I would talk and murmur to myself without paying attention to anyone else. I didn't care about anything. All day at school my head was elsewhere. I had a complete lack of interest in everything going on around me. I did not live in this world.

According to psychiatrists, I have (or at least I had) a condition called paraphrenia, which is the ability to be in this world and another one at the same time. I could be talking to you for example, while in my head, I'm somewhere else completely, at the same time. This would happen to me naturally, without any effort on my part.

Ever since I was a kid, if I could be off by myself without anyone messing with me, I'd shut myself up in the house. This time alone allowed me to leave, to go fully into my other world. If I couldn't shut myself up in the house, I'd go out walking. I walked a lot, I'd go to parks, to places where there weren't a lot of people. I could cross the street and avoid obstacles, but at the same time I was like a robot. Mentally I was elsewhere. At times my surroundings faded away.

(. . .)

I had terrible migraines. My family said I was faking it to get attention, but those headaches absolutely killed me. I had to shut myself up; any light or sound made it worse. Later on, here in jail, they discovered that it was a problem with my gallbladder. I still have terrible attacks every now and then.

Didn't they ever take you to a doctor before you were in jail?

No, my mother wasn't very into that. The only times she took me to a doctor, it was actually to see a homeopath. And even then it was kind of under sufferance; at that time I was often fainting at school and they forced her to do something.

(. . .)

I didn't like school, but I had those children's encyclopedias *Lo sé todo* (*I Know Everything*) and I spent all my time reading them. I also had the Larousse dictionary in four giant volumes, a really nice one with big pictures. In that dictionary, for every letter (let's say it was *A*, for example) they would start with a giant letter *A* up in the corner, and beneath it in smaller type, the same letter in different styles. One of these was the Egyptian version. I learned the Egyptian alphabet so I could write in hieroglyphics. I liked reading; I'd spend hours with that dictionary.

The problem with school was that I wasn't interested in anything. The answer to "school" was "no." No. I didn't go. I didn't study, I didn't do my homework. I'd run off, I wouldn't go to class, I'd be absent for two weeks at a time, a month even. I went walking instead, to think about my own things, in my own world.

(. . .)

Because I paid no attention to anything, I got the worst grades you could imagine, so of course I'd hide my report card for three months, which in turn meant that everything at school fell apart. When that happened, they called my mother, and then I had to face the consequences.

<u>What were the consequences?</u>

My mother would give me a real beating. She gave me plenty of terrible beatings. I tried to kill myself four times because of this.

<u>Could you tell me a bit more about that?</u>

They were dramatic, fantastical attempts.

<u>In what sense?</u>

I added in elements of all the little fantasies I played out, they were scenarios I had put together in my mind. For example, for my first attempt I drank methylated spirits. I drank the alcohol in a kind of ceremonial way and then lay down on my bed with my arms crossed over my chest, as if that way I'd be ready for the coffin.

<u>What happened?</u>

Nothing. I didn't even get sick. I burned my throat, that's for sure. I drank it pure without diluting it at all. I drank two full cups, and nothing happened. There's a sticker on it that says POISON, but it doesn't do anything. Then I swallowed a bottle of Cenestal pills.

<u>What's Cenestal?</u>

They were Mother's sleeping pills. They're little yellow pills—I swallowed about fifty of them. Then I slept for three days. After that I wanted to hang myself, but an aunt who lived next door saw me and started shouting, asking what the hell I was doing. The last time I thought about doing it was when I was twelve or thirteen years old, when I went up to the rooftop terrace on the Rawson Hotel, which is between Rawson and Lavalleja Streets. I climbed up there with the intention of jumping off, and I got right to the very edge, but once I was up there, it didn't seem like such a great idea.

<u>Why not?</u>

It seemed too violent. The mess, the impact. I didn't want to destroy myself.

<u>So who was this scene for, then?</u>

I didn't see it as a message for others. It was more for me.

<u>And how old were you during all of this?</u>

Eleven, twelve years old.

<u>Did you ever leave a note?</u>

No. There are some people who think, "If I won the lottery, all my problems would be solved." Well for me, it was always "I hope I die in my sleep." I just wanted someone to feel sorry for me while I passed over from one world to the next, asleep, in the most painless way possible. From sleep to death.

<u>After these attempts you made, how did your mother react?</u>

I never told her about them. I don't think she was ever fully aware.

<u>How could she fail to notice if you took fifty sleeping pills and slept for three days?</u>

She never gave a shit. We never had a loving relationship.

<u>Did you ever fantasize about shooting yourself?</u>

No. Never. Like I said, I was afraid of violence.

<u>Why did you stop trying to kill yourself?</u>

I stopped going to school. That was the source of everything.

<u>Was each attempt due to something at school?</u>

Absolutely. I never had the instinct for self-preservation. What do I mean by that? If you stick your fingers in an electrical socket, and you get a shock, you think about it for a moment, and you don't put your fingers in the socket again. If I was in the same fucked-up situation, I'd get to the point of trying to kill myself, I'd fail, I'd face up to my mother, and she'd beat the living daylights out of me, and then in three months the same thing would happen again. I had no instinct to save myself; I never learned from my mistakes.

Perhaps it's a bit more complicated than that?

I'm just trying to explain it in simple terms. Besides all that, karma is karma. If I was meant to die then, I would have died. If I didn't die, it's because for me, there was more to come.

3

When they arrested me, they put me in front of an expert—
the same expert doctor they used for Robledo Puch, "The
Angel of Death." This doctor spoke with me, with my family, and tried to sort of reconstruct my story. Then at one
point while we were chatting, the guy said to me, "Ricardo,
I saw your mother this week, and we had a long discussion . . . I know you don't know much about this sort of
thing, but didn't you ever think about having your mother
committed to a psychiatric hospital?"

<u>Why did he say that?</u>

It seems like during the discussion with my mother, she
went on a long rant that was all mystical. Another time, a
psychologist told me, "Ricardo, schizophrenics aren't born,
they're made. And your mother did everything she possibly could to make sure you ended up with a severe mental
disorder."

(. . .)

My mother thought that all men were botched abortions. She said it all the time. She was a very solitary woman, very paranoid about other people. She saw everyone as an enemy. I remember spending a lot of time alone: she would go to work and leave me locked up in the house. She locked me in because in her mind, people on the outside were all witches looking to hurt me. She was the only one who loved me, the only one who would always be there for me. These are all her words. In public she was always sweet as could be, but she didn't like other people. She had some friends, but they were all people she had met through her religion.

<u>What was her religion?</u>

She was a Spiritualist. There was a private chapel where she practiced Spiritualism. Their meetings were kind of clandestine. They took place at a chapel inside a private home, where there was no way to tell from the outside what was going on.

My mother said she became a Spiritualist because that's what fate had determined for her. She got caught up in all that nonsense when she was pregnant with me. She was just walking along the street when she began to feel unwell and sat down in the doorway of a particular building. The building happened to be the San Luis de Gonzaga Chapel, one of those private chapels with no signs indicating it's a place of worship. The people there welcomed her. They helped her and told her they had been waiting for her. She ended up becoming an important figure in that chapel. She took me there for many years.

How old were you at that time?

I was very young—she took me there from the moment I was born, I suppose.

What was the place like?

It was a large room that at one end had wooden benches upholstered in black, for the mediums, and in the room itself, there were benches a bit like church pews. They had a pitcher of water at the entrance, a huge pitcher that would be blessed by the presence of spirits, and then afterward you'd drink the energized water. We kids played outside in the yard, we just had to come back at the end to drink the water.

They gave you water that had been energized by the dead?

By the spirits, yes. Throughout the session the water would become energized, and then we drank it at the end.

The mediums sat on the benches up front. Each medium would be calm before the session began, but as the spirits took hold of them, their hands and feet would begin to tremble. When they stood up, it meant that the spirit had fully taken hold. There's always a link to movement. A Spiritualist doesn't dance, like in Umbanda, but they begin with a gesture of rubbing their legs to embody the spirit.

It was funny, because in my understanding of Spiritualism, it is a bit like Umbanda in that certain spirits appear in certain places, and there in our chapel of San Luis de Gonzaga de la Paternal we would often be visited by Sergeant Cabral, the hero of Argentine independence, or San Martín, the founding father. I could never understand why Sergeant Cabral showed up, in that particular spot. [*Melogno laughs.*] We never had any regular folks show up.

So, Sergeant Cabral and General San Martín . . . what did they have to say when they showed up?

They came to encourage good vibes, proper values . . . It was like they came to give their testimony, or to impart a lesson, really shady things. Nowadays, if I think back on those sessions, they don't seem that funny, to tell the truth.

(. . .)

One day, three of my mother's friends came to the house, and I was sent to my bedroom. After a while I began to hear loud noises, shouting, a real racket. I sneaked down to see what was going on: they'd made one of the old women kneel down on the ground while two more of them held her arms back, and then the rest took turns beating the evil out of her. It was quite a session of beatings, yelling, threats: the one woman with the spirit inside her thrashing about and shouting and trying to defend herself, and my mother and all the others beating her and shouting as well.

What sort of a beating was it?

Open-handed slaps, close-fisted punches as well. The woman kneeling on the floor had embodied the spirit of a woman who had hurt another woman.

<u>During the session?</u>

No. Beforehand. And they had summoned the spirit of that person to punish her, and to remove the pain. After all this, after a long period of time, after all the shouting and the slapping, they sat around together drinking tea, chatting away as if nothing had happened at all.

<u>Even the woman who had been slapped around?</u>

Even her. In their lives, that's how the rituals work.

<u>How can you tell if someone has embodied a spirit?</u>
<u>Does something change?</u>

No. Personally, I never noticed a physical change apart from the bit where they rub their legs and stand up. And in that chapel, they had little political intrigues among themselves as well, which is to say that they didn't always believe each other. They'd accuse someone of pretending, saying they hadn't embodied a spirit at all. They had resentments, gossip, and personal problems right there in their own chapel. It wasn't about money; it was more a question of personal power, of their position in a small, closed group. Many of the women were nasty characters, and now with a bit of distance, I can tell you that all the men were assholes.

(. . .)

For me, all this was normal. A kid who comes from a normal family, with a normal life, might have been able to realize that all this was very strange. I grew up in this environment, so it was natural. While I lived with her, my life with my mother seemed normal. I didn't know of any families who were living proper lives. For me, this was how the world was. It's not like I knew: "Everyone else is normal, but things are crazy here."

4

My mother used religion as a weapon: she beat the living daylights out of me, but she'd say it wasn't her who was beating me, it was God punishing me through her. She wasn't the kind of woman to use her hands—she always had a little stick, which was a piece of wood about this big [*Melogno uses his hands to indicate an object about a meter long and five centimeters in diameter*]. We called it "the little stick" because that's what she called it. She'd grab you by the neck and beat the shit out of you with the little stick. She beat us furiously; she went way too far. I'd wet myself sometimes with fear during those beatings.

Beyond the physical fear she instilled in me, I noticed that in her religious life outside the house, she was highly respected at her chapel. That's why on top of the beatings and the physical fear, there was also my spiritual fear of her. I was afraid of the house itself, even when my mother wasn't there.

In what sense?

There were things, spirits, in the house. When my mother locked me in, I walked around the house with a knife in my hand, because I was scared of all the things I could feel there.

So you're saying that on a daily basis, you would spend hours locked up in a house with spirits inside?

Yes. And if I had to get up during the night to use the bathroom, I'd wrap myself up in a sheet, for protection.

Why?

For self-defense. Now, many years later, I can tell you there's no logic to walking around with a knife to protect yourself from a spirit. What are you going to do with a knife, or a bedsheet? And then later on, when I had the gun . . . sleeping with a pistol locked and loaded beneath my pillow, I was more likely to end up with a bullet in my own brain than anything else. But in any case, these are the sorts of things that made me feel safer.

Did the spirits ever talk to you? Did you communicate with them?

No, never. I never saw them, either. I *felt* them. I felt them there.

Sometimes when people sense spirits, they get goose bumps or feel physical fatigue.

No, that's just fear. Imagine going down into a basement

and you know there's something there. Something more visceral than that. A constant tension in the face of something you can't see or touch. I felt the presence of spirits all the time; I checked under beds, behind doors and curtains. I felt them there.

Was there any special connection between your house and the mirrors, or clocks on the walls?

No. I figured my house was fairly normal, there weren't too many strange things about it. If someone came to visit, they wouldn't think religion was something predominant in the family. Mirrors have more to do with clairvoyance. In Unit 20, mirrors weren't allowed. Apart from the fact that you could break them up and use them as shivs, in a psychiatric sense there are many patients who can't look in the mirror. In religion, the mirror is used as an instrument of vision. Don't forget that the first clairvoyants saw things in water. You have to look at a mirror and keep staring until the image disappears. Which is another way of saying you stand in front of a mirror and stare until you erase yourself, you disappear from the mirror and you begin to see other things.

Did you have dreams, or nightmares?

Not that I can recall. I never remembered my dreams back then. I don't remember them now, either. Either I don't have dreams, or I don't remember them. Same goes with nightmares.

(. . .)

The spirits I could sense were the product of my mother's environment, and also a product of her own force. She used religion and mysticism as a way of putting pressure on me.

But it was me too.

It's very rare for spirits to physically manifest; it's rare that you can see them. If a spirit manifests it's either because it's a particularly strong spirit, or because it has serious unresolved business in this world. Or it could be because the person who beholds it is particularly sensitive to spirits. In all those places my mother took me . . . well, everyone said that I had this strong ability for channeling that I had inherited from her.

Besides the San Luis de Gonzaga Chapel, my mother took me to Brother Miguel's meetings. I saw him on TV the other day and I bet he's a huge asshole. But when I was a kid, I thought he was strong spiritually. My mother worked there. All the stars went to see him, Susana Giménez, the famous actress, Carlos Monzón, the boxing champion, those sorts of people, because he was a sort of famous healer, but for Spiritualists. A lot of people got caught up in it—buses full of people came from Plaza Flores straight to his temple, and there was a whole commercial side to it as well. All this was going on during the military dictatorship, when things like that were banned, so you can imagine just how powerful he must have been. He had brought together the best mediums in the country. During the ceremonies he was up in a pulpit, and behind him, all the mediums sat in rows of chairs, giving him strength to do his work. He would stand up in these huge rooms, full of people, and he would single someone out by saying, "You there, your problem is such and such, and the solution is such and such, now you can go," and then the guy would get up without saying a word and leave. And he would do that one by one until the room was empty. Then the room would fill up again, over and over again.

<u>What work did your mother do there?</u>

She was one of the mediums who sat behind him. I'm telling you this because one day Brother Miguel said to me, "Ricardito, you're very strong, you have an, um, huge capacity . . . it's a shame you're marked for the other side."

<u>Why did he say that?</u>

I can't remember why. I remember he was very serious when he told me that: you're marked for the other side. I just stared back at him, barely understanding.

<u>How old were you then?</u>

Seven or eight years old.

Another time, when I was older—when my father had set me up in the bread and milk distribution business, there was a woman, a big Uruguayan woman with a huge behind who split the rent on the place with my father and had set up a kiosk there. One day this woman brought a healer in from the country, a guy a lot like the old medicine man Pancho Sierra with his poncho and flowing beard, you know, a real country type. She brought him in to bless her store: that was fairly common at the time, to cleanse the energy of the place so business would go well. This took place on a Monday, while my business was closed, but as I was living in a room behind the store, the woman knocked at my door and told me to open up so I could receive a blessing too. So I got dressed and opened the door to the store. The healer came in, took one look around, and immediately wanted to leave, shaking his head with a sort of revulsion. The Uruguayan woman was a little taken aback, and asked him what was wrong. But the only thing the healer would say was "No, no, let's leave." And there was nothing strange in the store, nothing strange in sight. A few days later I ran into the woman and she told me: "That man I brought to your store is a healer, but he didn't want to bless your business because he saw a great darkness, something very dense inside you."

These were some of the external signs that showed me I had a dark side.

5

I had a dog, a Pomeranian crossed with something else, that I found in the street. I wanted to call her Benji (it was around the time the movie *Benji* came out) but in the end she was called Juana, because my mother said, "She's going to be called Juana." She used to call me "Juana" as well. She called the three of us brothers "girls." And she called me Juana. She accepted my bringing the dog home, but she treated her very poorly. She would beat the dog with the same stick she used to beat us. And that thing I told you about how all men are botched abortions? That came from one time when my mother was beating the dog and my eldest brother tried to defend her. That's when my mother came out with it: all men are botched abortions.

Later, there was a cat, the poor thing. I was pretty nasty to that cat.

Because of all the problems I got into at school, at one

point my mother sent me to live with this sort of boyfriend she had, who was a doorman at the Rawson Hotel. That's the hotel I told you about where I went to see about jumping off the roof. That all happened when I was living there.

<u>Why did she do that?</u>

What?

<u>Send you to live with someone else?</u>

Because of all the shit around sending me to school. I think they knew each other through religion. The guy was a Spiritualist too, someone from the same part of the countryside as her. Opposite the hotel there was a Catholic school, and the boyfriend sent me there during the week and I went home to my mother's place on the weekends.

So, my mother brought this cat home. Then the cat began to take my place. My mother had it castrated. The cat took my spot, the son of a bitch. So, whenever I went home, I tortured the cat as much as I could. I'd put it in the freezer. Or I'd grab it by the scruff of the neck, its legs dangling in the air, and then I'd pull its tongue while I yanked its head the other way. Things like that. The poor cat was terrified of me. As soon as he saw me he'd dash off to hide on the roof. Afterward he couldn't get down. He'd climb the walls and stay up there meowing, and then the only way to get him down was with a ladder, a real fucking mess. That's when my mother put a collar on him, tied to a leash, and at the end of the leash she attached a roller bearing this big [*Melogno makes a circle twenty centimeters in diameter with his hands*] so that he couldn't get away. The cat spent his life dragging that heavy roller bearing around. You'd know the cat was nearby from the sound of the roller bearing being dragged along, or because he got tangled around the legs of the furniture. And you know what? From all that time dragging the bearing along, the cat's legs grew massive. He looked like some kind of beast.

I don't know what happened afterward to the cat. When I left home my mother gave the dog away. I know she went to a good home. But I don't know what happened to the cat.

Where did that cat come from? Did she find it?

No, she bought it.

So, what you're saying is, as soon as you left home, your mother bought a cat, had it castrated, and then tied it to a roller bearing that weighed two kilos?

Yeah. You see, my mother had this sort of perverse obsession with ownership and control.

I wasn't allowed to have friends, and no one could come and visit me either, because according to her, anyone from the outside could hurt me. As I got a little older, I began to see how she was grooming me to be the submissive son who cares for her in her old age.

(. . .)

Once we were at my godmother's place, an apartment in the city center. She was a nurse at the Borda Hospital and she was a Spiritualist too. They went out—who knows what they were up to—and I was left with my godmother's son, who must have been, let's say, twenty-five years old. After a while a girl he worked with came over, because they had something they had to do, a work thing, nothing strange. I just sat there in silence, without interfering, while they chatted. A few hours went by and my mother and godmother came back. My godmother started asking her son who this girl was, why she was there. So he started explaining but she cut him off and said, "I told you never to bring anyone here!" Then she slapped him across the face. Right in front of the girl. This was a defining moment in my adolescence. I saw that and my immediate thought was, "If this sucker is still getting slapped around at twenty-five years of age, what's going to happen to me?" And I said to myself, "I'm getting out of here, no matter what."

(. . .)

To get free of my mother, I began to study Santería.

The thing is, when it came to my mother, apart from physical fear, I also had this religious fear. I tried to gain knowledge in Spiritualism to get one over on my mother, but even my mother's Spiritualist friends told me, "You're crazy, you'll never get anywhere like this." But there were others who had the clarity to tell me, "Look, we'll set you on this other path and you'll be fine." So, they sent me to Brazil and I entered into Santería. But I never did it because of faith; I did it as a tool to fight my mother. I needed strength to confront her.

How old were you around this time?

Thirteen, fourteen years old.

<u>And how were these people connected to your mother?</u>

They were friends through her religion, other Spiritu-alists. There was some contact between Spiritualism and Santería, they were two sides of the same coin, in certain respects.

<u>Why did you have to go to Brazil?</u>

Because there's no Santería in Argentina. I spent nearly a month in Búzios. I went to meetings, I joined the cult. I was baptized in blood. I made ground.

<u>What does "make ground" mean?</u>

Santería is not like those evangelical churches where you rock up and say "I accept Jesus Christ" and right then and there they dip you in the water to baptize you and it's all done. With Santería, I spent several days in a com-pletely dark room, spread out on the floor, to purify myself. In the initiation process for Santería it's not the group of people who have to accept you. The spirits have to accept you: you are presented before them, and just as easily as they can accept you, they can also reject you, and bounce you off the walls. I was baptized in blood. They gave me my patron saints, the ones who would guide me and give me strength.

<u>What type of blood was it?</u>

Blood from a black rooster. They hold it above your head when they kill it, so the blood runs over you.

<u>Do they give you a new name during the initiation?</u>

No. They give you your patron saints. A spirit can accept you and help you, but if not, it can treat you really bad.

<u>And who speaks to you?</u>

The spirits take control of the *pai*, a kind of priest, and speak to you.

<u>Did the spirits speak to you?</u>

Yes. But I couldn't understand a word; it was some ancient language.

<u>Does the trance produce any physical changes in a person?</u>

Yes, that's the most noticeable thing. The transformation is very obvious. You see it and you realize that there's something else right in front of you, you're no longer the same. It's very dramatic.

<u>And how did you deal with all this? You were quite young.</u>

The need and longing I felt was stronger than any fear. You do things for a reason. You don't think about what you're doing, you think about the end goal.

Santería, Umbanda, Voodoo, and other religions were brought by slaves from Africa, and these slaves were depressed, they lived in captivity. So, you can imagine they didn't use their religion to bless the master's crops. Religion was for self-defense and revenge. Which is understandable.

For me it was quite special, because at that time it gave me the strength to face up to my greatest fear. When I came back from Brazil, I was full of strength and it was just the little shove I needed to go to my mother and say, "That's enough." I got home and the next day I told her. And then I left. Without any explanation, I told her I was leaving, and that was it.

(. . .)

And then afterward, how did religion continue to affect your life?

It didn't. I achieved my goal and I didn't mess with religion again for a long time after that. I took it up again when I went to jail, more as a way of defending myself, of surviving.

Other people have said they saw darkness inside you. What did your mother think of that?

Nothing at all. To her I was a cockroach, a piece of garbage. But she saw nothing dark or negative in me.

One of the theories from the forensic medical team was that if I'd killed my mother, I never would have committed the crimes.

Do you think that's true?

I don't think so.

Did you ever fantasize about killing your mother?

No. Never.

When did you see her last?

When I was twenty years old. For some strange reason I went over to her house, and when I got there, she was with a boyfriend. She had started going out with an evangelical and they were going to get married. In a very formal manner, the guy asked me for my mother's hand in marriage. A crazy idea like that could only have come from her. When I was arrested, my mother was on her honeymoon in Mar del Plata.

Do you ever wonder if she's still alive today?

No. I don't care. If one day I can have a life again, I want to start over; I don't want to have anything to do with any of that. I don't want family, I don't want anything. I just want to be left alone.

6

Whenever I imagine a group of people meeting together, I always imagine myself in the darkest possible corner, happy to watch everything. From the outside. In my own world, I was always the protagonist, and even if I was stuck in that dark corner, everyone else was beholden to what I was doing there. In real life, I was still in the dark corner, but nobody paid me any attention.

(. . .)

There was one psychiatrist who said it wasn't a case of my having no emotions. I had emotions, but my emotional education as an individual had been so insignificant that I didn't think emotions had anything to do with me. Maybe that's where my alternative world came from. In that other world I had everything I needed, and here I had nothing. Here I felt no desire, no sense of the future, nothing.

<u>What did you do in that other world?</u>

I made my own films: I imagined the scenes, putting together bits and pieces of the same stories. Which is to say, I'd relive the TV shows and films I had seen in my head, with myself as the main character. I'd spend the whole day doing this. For example, I was obsessed with *Shogun* for about a year. I spent the whole year reliving the story, reconstructing it scene by scene, changing little things like the dialogue or the ending. I can still remember the characters: there was Mariko, and Toranaga, who was the leader. I would take on the role of the main character and tweak it as I wanted. Some scenes would get me so worked up I would cry. That's how deeply re-creating these stories affected me. I'd take a secondary character and live out their story too.

<u>What sort of changes would you make?</u>

It would depend on how I felt that day. I would take a problem from this world and resolve it in the fantasy world. I also used comics this way, I was obsessed with *El Tony, Fantasía, D'Artagnan . . .*

<u>These were all comic books from Editorial Columba. They had a whole universe of stories. There was also *Nipur de Lagash, Savarese, Gilgamesh the Immortal, Black Eagle, Mark, Or-Grund, Chindits, Jackaroe . . .*</u>

These were the most important things in my life—I'd wait for the kiosk to open so I could get the latest issues. One of the most important characters for building stories in my head was Dax, because I was obsessed with the

Far East. Dax was blind and had supernatural powers. It was set in the time of the Widower Empress in China, the Boxer Rebellion, a time of revolution and upheavals. Dax had French parents but he had been raised in China. He was blind but he could hypnotize people and he had tele-kinetic powers.

(...)

Mark was an important character too. He lived in a post-apocalyptic time; the world had been destroyed by nu-clear warfare and the survivors tried to make things from the rubble while fighting off the mutants.

Do you remember Mark's sidekick?

Yes ... um, Hawk, wasn't it?

Do you remember he had a strange arm?

A cybernetic arm.

No, it was a mutant arm.

Yes, but they'd sort of covered it with this metal sleeve, so that the mutation couldn't spread. Without the sleeve, the mutation would spread and he'd become a mutant.

The whole time he was caught in this struggle between humanity and the encroaching mutants. He found his equilibrium.

What do you mean equilibrium? Eventually the metal sleeve stopped working and he turned into a full mutant.

Oh, I forgot about that.

Yeah. Well, there's an episode where Hawk loses con-trol of his metal arm and becomes a mutant forever.

(. . .)

I also used movies. I really liked *Scanners*, for example, I loved those mental powers . . .

<u>There was a time when I used to fantasize about being Darth Vader while I talked to my colleagues at work. I'd be chatting with them but in my head I'd be watching them fall down dead right in front of me, just like in *Star Wars.*</u>

For me, my whole life was more or less like that, except for one big difference. You talk about imagining those things to escape being in the moment. I was *already out* of the moment. That state of mind came naturally to me. I would drift off.

Between these two worlds there was a huge level of dissociation. I crossed over because I was much happier on the other side. If I could have found food and shelter there I would have stayed. I would never have come back.

In some ways, everyone lives in a fantasy world. Buying a lottery ticket is living a fantasy. But it's a normal fantasy. Normal fantasies always have a wall around them, something that stops you from crossing over to the other side. I didn't have that, there was nothing to stop me. If I hadn't been arrested . . . I believe that because of the way I was living my life, unmoored from the real world, I believe that by the age of twenty-five I would have killed myself.

<u>Why?</u>

Because I couldn't cope. The real world demands attention. If you don't pay attention to the real world, you lose it. And the other world doesn't provide a way of living, you can't live there. Because it's one thing to live in a fantasy world when you're a teenager, but it's something else entirely when you're an adult and you have to perform a job or live with a family, pay attention to this and that. If you spend your whole day in this parallel world you'll end up ruined, as lonely as a paving stone, or living in the street. And let me tell you this: I've had my time with drugs here.

Here in jail?

Yes, I used drugs for the first time in jail. I really like cannabis; I think it's the best drug there is. I took Artane for a number of years, because it provided a very heavy hallucinatory state, and that allowed me to stay awake, to have fun and crack myself up laughing. But I never—well, there was one time I took Rohypnol, and I never took it again. Rohypnol is a hypnotic. It's that infamous drug where a guy who's taken it wakes up in jail and has no idea what happened, or what he did. It's a total blackout. The one time I took it I blacked out and the next day people told me the things I'd done and I had no memory of it. That's why I never took it again. I don't allow anything to take away my sense of control over my own actions.

For someone like me, who did such terrible things the last time I lost control, I can't allow that to happen again. Because of my actions, because of the deaths I caused, I'm very afraid of a world in which I lose control.

(. . .)

I didn't seek out the fantasy world; I would wake up and I'd already be there. It was natural. That's another reason I never questioned it, because for me it was natural. The questioning of this other world began in jail, and I'd have to say only after being in jail for a long time. It took a lot of medication and treatment to get me out of that world. For me it was something I thought would be there for my whole life, but over the years in jail, I was given preventative treatments, heavy stuff, all kinds of therapy and serious medications. And my fantasy world began slipping away. One day, when I must have been thirty-six or thirty-seven years old, I noticed that the world was gone forever. It's like waking from a dream you want to get back to, but when you go looking for it, you realize it's too late. You're awake. And you ask yourself, "What happened? What happened to me?" I thought it would last my whole life, because in jail a fantasy world is a wonderful tool, almost a necessity to mentally escape from where you've been confined.

There's a report they made about me years ago, in 2005, I believe. In that report they said something like there's a parallel part of me that I can't quite unify with reality, and that whenever I faced a difficulty I would escape to that place. By then my fantasy world was practically nonexistent; my imagination was more or less extinguished after so many years of haloperidol and all the other medication.

<u>At any time with these fantasies you've told me about, was there anything related to killing?</u>

No. I want to emphasize this point very clearly: I never fantasized about *killing*. In my little films I was the good guy, the hero—I was never the bad guy, the murderer. My fantasy world could perhaps . . . have you seen *Las puertitas del Señor López* [a 1988 Argentine film about a spineless everyman who works for a large company and escapes his reality "mentally" when he passes through bathroom doors]? In that movie, López was at the center of his own fantasies; he was the main character. My world was more like that, you could say. No matter what the fantasy was, I was the protagonist. In the real world, I was never the protagonist. In my fantasy world, I didn't imagine killing people or torturing them. I fantasized about being a person, which I never was in real life.

7

When I left my mother's place, I rented an apartment in Lomas del Mirador, right by my father's house. He helped me sign the contract, because I was a minor. I started secondary school, but I quit. For a while I worked in a big warehouse, then with my old man, making shoes. It was a good job. I had a good life.

My life was becoming manageable, calm.

I studied electronics for two years at a private college, in Flores, to become a repairman for domestic appliances. I had a yoga phase; I did martial arts and all those East Asian things. I also tried to join the navy. I applied to join the school for navy mechanics, but they rejected me.

<u>Why?</u>

I didn't pass the test. I flunked the psychological part. It was stupid, the test. They gave you these plaques with numbers on them that were inside little balls. I can't really remember exactly. But I couldn't find the right numbers.

But then I had to do military service. I was sent to the 601st Battalion, in Villa Martelli.

<u>And how did things work out there?</u>

I spent the whole time in jail.

<u>Why?</u>

There was a problem with weapons in our unit. Because I'd been working in shoemaking, they made me a leather worker. I repaired holsters, belts, anything made of leather, and my work station was in the arsenal. I knew that two of my fellow soldiers were stealing weapons. But I didn't turn them in. In the arsenal there were personal weapons that had been left there that belonged to officials who were away on commission. Those two soldiers would steal absolutely anything they could sell. They even stole one of the officer's ceremonial swords. So eventually those two were arrested and I went down with them, because I knew what they'd been doing and I kept my mouth shut. There were four of us. They paraded us in front of the troops as "subversives," but those idiots were no guerrillas, they were just delinquents. I spent the rest of my military service in the unit's jail. I was locked up for over a year without release. I missed the whole Malvinas conflict because of it. Then, after the war, a military tribunal reopened my case and determined that I was guilty of concealing a crime, and they let me out under this system where I had to come back to the regimental headquarters every so often, dressed in my uniform.

<u>Did you shoot a weapon during your training?</u>

I learned how to take apart a gun, how to shoot, yeah.

<u>What weapons did you shoot?</u>

An FAL assault rifle, and then an FAP. Because I was a good shot, they made me a marksman with the FAP rifle. What other weapons did I shoot? 357 revolvers, .38 Special revolvers, Bataan shotguns. Any time they wanted to test a weapon we went to the bottom of the barracks where there was a little stream, a large gorge, and a sort of trash heap where we'd do our shooting. I did a lot of shooting there. I know how to take apart an FAL and clean it.

<u>Is it hard? Does it have a lot of pieces?</u>

You only take apart the bits you need to clean. You have to take out the gas port, which has a spring underneath, and the slide. It's not like you have to take the whole rifle apart. There are fifteen pieces. You oil them, clean them, then put them back together. After a while they made you do it with your eyes closed.

(. . .)

<u>How did you deal with your fantasy world during military service?</u>

On that front there were no problems at all. There's a special term we use during military service: *acovacharse*. It's when you're ordered to go and do something, and you slink off and go and hide somewhere instead. Then there's "standing guard." "Standing guard" is when you're sent to a post in the middle of nowhere for hours at a time until you're relieved, and you have no radio or TV or anything, you're just out there on your own like an idiot, with a loaded FAL assault rifle. For me that was perfect. There are lots of jobs like that during military service, jobs where you just stand there for hours on end doing nothing. It's not like they get the conscripts to design nuclear submarines. When all you have to do is run, do frog jumps, push-ups . . . you push your body, but your mind is elsewhere. As long as your body can keep up, it's fine: you don't have to be there.

Even today, you can see that the guards here in jail spend the whole day on their phones with their messages and little games, all that nonsense. For me, the phone and the little games were all in here. [*Melogno taps his head.*]

(. . .)

The doctors say that having my life organized by others is a container that keeps me safe. Military service is a bit like that—you have a container, an order, a structure you have to move around in. That's what the doctors said, anyway. I spent two years in a structured world during my military service. It's a structured world that for better or worse is a system that boxes you in and maintains you. I spent two years like that. Then all of a sudden, I was on the outside. I spent two months in the real world and then . . . what a nightmare.

8

I have a story. This story has many gaps in it, gaps that have been filled along the way by forensic experts, psychiatrists, doctors. I accept that others filled in my story for me. And those gaps then became solid parts of reality. I reconstruct my acts through the words of others, I reconstruct time through other people's chronologies, because if you were to ask me, I have no conception of time in that moment. I pieced my story together through what I can remember and what others have told me.

There are flashes, explosions, things stuck in my memory, but at the same time I ask myself: "Did that happen or not?" Which is to say, for me it's recorded in my head as a memory, but I'm not sure if it happened in this world, or if it happened in the other one and I've brought it over. It might also be something someone told me and I think it's a memory.

(. . .)

The essential problem with that time in my life is that I simply wasn't there. Not long ago, a psychiatrist read some things to me from a file they had. Many things weren't as I remembered them. There were memories that weren't quite right or that I remembered differently. Time was dislocated in tiny details.

<u>You got out of military service after the Malvinas War. The war ended in the middle of June [1982], you got out in July, and the murders happened before the end of September. Two and half months, more or less.</u>

When I got out of military service, it was a bit like coming back and starting from zero. I had been working since I was fourteen, most recently with my father making shoes in the workshop. But when I get out of military service there was less work—in fact, there was hardly any. A lot of people were really struggling to get by. Because of this, my father helped me out and set me up with a business, a little store selling bread and milk.

I looked after the store, I had my routine; I worked until eight in the evening, then closed up, had something to eat, and then I'd go for a walk. I'd walk for hours in Mataderos, Flores, Liniers. I'd cross over into Buenos Aires Province. I walked like a dog. I wandered about kind of randomly. Sometimes I'd do several laps of a short circuit.

<u>What do you mean by that?</u>

For example, I might walk around the same block fifty times.

The same block?

Yes.

(...)

Everything felt very . . . distant, very meaningless. I can't remember anything that excited me; there was nothing, not even music. I remember I watched TV, but that too felt very distant.

I preferred walking at night, because everything was calmer. It made my automatism easier; there were fewer people who looked at me, everything was more fluid. In any case, I preferred to lock myself up at home to be in my own world. In the streets I set that world inside my head free, but I felt guilty about it, because I knew it wasn't normal. Which is to say, there was a sense of guilt attached to that freedom. In the streets I had to be careful about talking to myself. I was very ashamed of talking to myself and gesticulating, and when someone caught me doing it I had to hide it, I'd start humming or something, as if I were singing a song.

Why did that upset you?

Pure and simple, it upset me anytime anyone looked at me. I didn't like feeling watched. Even if no one was watching me, I still felt like . . . yes, like I was the object of everyone's staring.

Why is that?

I don't know. There was no specific reason. It was like an instinct, something that was generated inside my body.

Maybe for someone looking in from the outside, that seems strange. Something closer to shame or paranoia. The shame that comes from being watched. It physically upset me to think of people watching me. That's what paranoia is, I think.

Can you remember any anecdotes from your time at the bread store?

No, not really. I wished nobody would come. I hated serving customers.

How did you come to be living in the streets?

In those days, bakeries were shut on Mondays, so there was no bread for me to sell in my store. One Monday I went out walking, and when I returned home, I realized that I had no desire for anything. I spent the whole day out walking, going around and around the neighborhood, and when night came and it was time to return home, I realized I didn't want to go. It was like I was a kid watching television at night and I'd been told it was time for bed. What can I say? *I didn't want to go home.* I wanted to keep walking. I didn't want to be anywhere. I didn't want to open the store again. I didn't want anything. There was nowhere I wanted to be. So I went and took the cash from the store and the pistol, and I left a note for my father on the counter: I said that I was fine, and that I was leaving. I didn't take any of my things with me; the only thing I wanted was to leave.

Why did you want to leave?

There was no "why." I just wanted to leave. Leave, leave,

leave. It was like I was leaving one place but I wasn't going anywhere else. Nowhere.

So I started living in the streets. I slept in Alberdi Park, which is in Mataderos, opposite the police precinct that later on spent the most time looking for me. During the day I wandered around, occasionally eating in the neighborhood pizzerias. I slept in the park, or sometimes in the cinema, where I would pay for one movie and stay all afternoon. I went to the cinema in San Martín de Flores, or in Liniers, theaters where they kept playing films on a loop. I'd go in the afternoon and come out at midnight. I'd watch the same movie all day, all week, until they changed what was showing. They were cheap theaters with the movies on a loop, the ushers didn't bother you, you had a roof over your head, and it was dark and safe. When it rained, I'd take the subway and sleep while the train went from one end of the line to the other. My days went by like clockwork. Everything was kind of unreal. I'd walk, I'd drift.

<u>Did you wash, keep yourself clean, and so on?</u>

I'd use the bathrooms in bars and pizzerias. To properly bathe and rest I'd occasionally go for a night to a shed my father had behind his house; he kept things from his shoemaking business there, piles of old leather and things like that. I knew it was always unlocked, and I'd hide away there. It had a bathroom where I could clean myself up a little, although it's not like I paid too much attention to that sort of thing anyway. Sometimes I'd sleep there too, in the warehouse.

(. . .)

In general, I'd sort of doze. I didn't sleep because I always had to be alert in case anyone came.

<u>Why were you worried about that?</u>

Because of people. You know there are people out there. And your instincts keep you alert to what's out there. Even if there's no real threat posed by the people around you, you're still on the alert.

Still, there were times when I'd fall into a deep sleep in a square, after hours and hours of aimlessly wandering. I'd get so tired I practically collapsed. Sometimes I'd get bored and I'd go into a bar and watch television.

<u>What do you mean when you say you got bored?</u>

Going to a bar meant having access to a television, and that provided some kind of world for me, because in the street there was nothing. There comes a time when the machinery needs a break.

<u>The machinery: was that you?</u>

My mind.

<u>So what you're saying is, you'd get to a certain point where what was inside your head wasn't enough, you felt like you were lacking something?</u>

Yes.

<u>And in those moments where you felt a lack, what were you thinking? Did that make you question anything?</u>

No. Besides, it didn't happen very often. But sometimes I'd turn the same thing over in my head so many times that I got bored; my brain would shift down a couple of gears and so would I. These moments forced me into a kind of void, where there was nothing I could do. And that boredom was also like a kind of peace. I would sit on a bench in the square and watch the old folks feeding the pigeons, that sort of thing.

That mental state—do you think you came out of military service like that? Could you trace perhaps not an origin, but a progression, a growth in that kind of mental state?

No. It's not like I came out of military service in a bad state. I went in there like that.

Can you recall any particular stress at that time that might have led to . . . ?

Ahhh . . . no. Stress is the biggest load of bullshit this century, in my day there was no such thing as stress.

OK, let me ask if you were in a particularly unsettled state . . .

If I'd been in some kind of unsettled state, that would have rung some kind of alarm, something would have alerted me. No. I don't remember feeling unsettled.

In the newspapers there was an article about a neighbor who said he saw you a few days before you were arrested, and that you told him that you had "a problem inside." Do you remember that conversation?

No. [*Melogno looks at a copy of* Gente *with a photo of the neighbor.*] Oh yes, I remember that guy. He was an old man who lived in the neighborhood. But I don't remember speaking to him back then.

If you had to define your mental state during that month in one word, what would it be?

Absent. Limbo.

This should give you an idea of what it was like: when I started living in the streets, my shoes broke from so much walking, so I bought some cheap boots. I liked them so I bought them. But they were a bit tight on me, the inside of the boot was very narrow. So, from all my walking I got a pretty nasty blister on the bottom of my foot. When that blister burst open into a sore, I don't remember feeling any pain. I walked around with that open sore for hours and hours every day, for over twenty days. Then later when I was arrested, they took my boots off—they're not allowed in jail—gave me some sandals, and began to heal my foot. I knew I had hurt myself, because I can the remember the wound getting better and that it took a long time. But I have no memory of the pain, or any consciousness of walking with that pain. I don't remember feeling anything.

9

<u>How much time passed between you going to live in the streets and the first murder?</u>

A week, I think. Maybe two.

<u>How did it happen?</u>

I'd spent the whole afternoon dozing in the Grand Liniers Cinema, which had two screens split over two floors, right next to Avenida General Paz. I left the cinema and stood outside on the corner of the street that continues down onto Avenida Rivadavia. I must have stood there for a couple of hours, like someone waiting for a bus, watching people walk by, lost in my world, until an internal desire said to me, "the next taxi." And so I flagged down the next taxi to pass by. I gave the driver a random address, and when we arrived I didn't know where he had ended up; it was the last place I would have expected, near the San Pantaleón church in Lomas del Mirador.

He was a patron saint of the sick. How did you remember it was the San Pantaleón church?

Because as we drove by I saw the church in the dark. I was chatting away calmly with the guy, no problems.

Talking about what?

Just chitchat. The weather, the night. You get the picture; I was just a kid with a dopey-looking face.

When you gave him the address, did you know you were going to kill him?

Yes.

In the meantime, what were you thinking about? Do you remember anything about how you were feeling in that moment?

No. I don't think I could say that I had any type of feeling in the moment. I remember that to get from Liniers to where we were, the guy took the highway and then Avenida General Paz to get to La Tablada, and he was supposed to take the first exit, but instead he stayed on and took the second exit, which made the trip longer. He told me he wasn't taking the long way to try to rip me off, it was because at the first exit there was a military roadblock where they were checking vehicles, so he took the second exit so they wouldn't bust his balls.

We got to our destination, he stopped the car and turned around to tell me how much I owed, and that's when I shot him. I closed my eyes when I pulled the trigger. I never wanted to see the man's face. When I opened my eyes again, he'd already fallen down. I reached over the seat and pulled him up, because he'd slumped over to the passenger side. I always let the person slump over, I never looked at their face, never looked at their eyes. That was the only time I was afraid. After I pulled the body back up, there was a moment of fear, of . . . terror. Suddenly I looked up and I saw that I was being watched. I didn't see a person, or a face. I saw two eyes that were watching me. I was paralyzed with fear until a few moments went by and I realized what was happening: it was the rearview mirror. They were my own eyes, in the rearview mirror. My own face, reflected. I didn't recognize myself. My eyes, my face. It was like there was a complete stranger right in front of me.

And your own eyes were watching you.

Yes. But just because when I looked up the mirror was right there, that doesn't mean this was some kind of mystical moment. The mirror just happened to be there. It's just that I couldn't recognize my own face, I didn't know my own reflection.

What was it about seeing your own eyes that startled you?

I was frightened by that staring, right in front of me. Yes, that's it . . . well, yes: I was frightened by the staring, right there in front of me. Suddenly discovering that *I was being watched*. You can't look too deeply into it for an explanation, because once I realized it was the mirror, I said to myself, "You're an idiot." That was the end of it; it's not like I spent time afterward thinking about it. Later on, psychiatrists told me that it's very common during psychotic episodes. No matter how physically present you are, you simply aren't living the moment. That's all it was. I didn't recognize my own reflection.

Then I looked at the guy again. I checked his pockets, I saw there was blood coming from his ears and nose, and then I realized he was dead. I remember thinking, "Is that it? Something as stupid as that?"

(. . .)

How stupid killing seemed.

How did you arrive at those thoughts?

Because of how easy it was. How simple the act itself was. There are also these societal expectations, what you see in movies, that if you shoot someone and kill them, you'll feel bad, you'll vomit, you'll have this huge oh-no-what-have-I-done moment. I felt none of that; I didn't feel any of those things that you're supposed to feel, I just thought, "Is that it?" There was no special feeling of pleasure, or fear . . . nothing. I don't remember feeling anything.

And afterward?

After that, I turned off the engine, leaned back and got comfortable in the seat, then I lit a cigarette. I sat in the car for ten, fifteen minutes, to take in the safety of death, smoking. Smoking without inhaling.

What do you mean by the safety of death?

Ah, how can I explain it? In some sense, that's where my mind went.

<u>What time was this?</u>

Around eleven at night. Thirty meters away there was a kiosk, people were standing there buying things.

<u>And you just stayed there for a while, with the car switched off.</u>

Yes.

<u>Was the radio in the taxi switched on?</u>

No, there was total silence.

<u>And while you were you sitting there, what were you thinking about?</u>

I don't know. When I say "I felt nothing" I should clarify: maybe I did feel something, but I have no reliable memory of it to tell you. I can tell you about the thing with the eyes in the rearview mirror because it's burned into my memory. But there's no record of feelings; I don't remember having felt anything. Perhaps staying in the car for fifteen minutes was a moment of peace, you could say. A calm after the explosion. But in any case, I have no memory of that. I just thought of that now.

<u>You got into the taxi knowing you were going to kill the driver. Did the fact that he told you he was taking the long way to avoid a military checkpoint change your thought process at all? Did it impact your decision?</u>

No, on the contrary, it made me feel even more sure, because—well, the guy could have taken a route where they checked the car. They would have found the gun and arrested me. But then he took a route to charge me more money, and he told me that right to my face. You say to yourself, "Shit, this guy deserves to die." That's where this theory I had for a while comes from, this idea that everything happens for a reason, that there had to be a "why."

And what would that reason be?

Fate. I thought it was fated that those people would die.

Is that what you thought in the moment?

No. I thought of it afterward. I thought it and said it later, when people asked me about it. While it was happening, I wasn't thinking anything.

What did you do afterward?

I got out of the car and went to Mataderos. I figure I must have walked about fifty blocks, to the bar where I would eat at night.

And what was that walk like?

I was like a robot, the same as always. I wasn't thinking about what had happened. I walked all the way to the Los Dos Hermanos bar, which was on the corner of Directorio and Larrazábal Streets. At that bar they've known me since I was a kid because I lived two blocks away. I went there all the time. I went there and ordered a *suprema napolitana* [chicken cutlet with cheese and marinara sauce on top] and fries, and then for dessert I had a Balcarce chocolate mousse. Chocolate mousse is one of the desserts I like the most. Chocolate is my real favorite, or dulce de leche eaten by the spoonful, but it has to be heavy dulce de leche, the type you use for baking.

So anyway, I ate there and watched some TV. By then it was almost midnight, and back then they stopped transmitting at midnight, or one at the very latest. The programs they put on at that time were pretty boring. Then I left the bar, walked for a while longer, and went to the Alberdi Park to sleep.

The first killing was an isolated act, so it kind of went by unnoticed. When I committed my killings in Mataderos things blew up, because it was three acts in a short space of time in a small area.

<u>Before that first act, did you ever have the impulse to kill?</u>

No.

<u>And when you say, "It must have occurred to me earlier?"</u>

I'm looking for . . . I'm also trying to find an explanation that seems satisfactory and reasonable. So when I say it must have occurred to me earlier, I say that because it's not possible that it came to me in the previous five seconds. I figure there must have been *something* beforehand that led me to what I did. Some sign, some warning. I don't want . . . I can't find . . . this isn't . . . in all these years, I haven't been able to find where the idea came from, where the need came from. I can't tell you how or when it occurred to me. Some of the experts thought it might have come from all the movies I had watched, or one of the movies I put together in my own head.

<u>Do you remember what movie you watched that evening?</u>

It was a movie with Franco Nero in it, *Hitch-Hike*. But I don't think—I don't think the idea came to me on the evening itself. I believe it must have come beforehand.

<u>You didn't get the idea while you were watching the movie?</u>

No, something is telling me that the answer here is no. At the same time, though, I didn't fantasize about killing. I don't know how to explain it. But it was already there, somehow. The idea was already there.

<u>Did you have the gun on you when you left the cinema?</u>

Yes, but I always had it with me. I carried it in a kind of leather bag like an envelope that was popular at the time. The pistol was the only thing I took with me when I left the house. I carried it around in the bag, and when I slept in the street, I used the bag as a pillow. The pistol was locked and loaded.

10

The second act took place on Pola Street, in the early morning of Thursday, September 23. How much time passed between the first and second killings? I couldn't find the exact date of the first crime.

It's possible that there was a day or two between them. But I think the second one happened the night after the first. If I'm not wrong, they happened on consecutive nights.

Where did you get in the second taxi?

In Liniers, fifteen or twenty minutes away from Mataderos. Of that particular act, the only thing I remember is that when I shot the guy, there was a house, let's say about four or five meters away, and through the window I could see the family eating dinner. You had the sidewalk, a little wall and a garden, and then a little bit farther up was the house. The windows were closed but the curtains were open, and I could see them all seated around the table for dinner. Two kids, the father, and then the mother standing there dishing out the food.

<u>Almost like an advertisement for the perfect family. What did you think when you saw that? There has to be a reason why you remember it.</u>

Yes . . . [*Melogno pauses for a few seconds.*] I understand there are some great unknowns in all this. I figure that something must have gone through my head, but I don't know if I forgot what it was or if I paid no attention to it at the time.

<u>Did you notice the family before or after shooting?</u>

During the shooting.

Afterward, everything was the same. I turned off the car, stayed inside for a while smoking one or two cigarettes with the driver slumped over. Then I got out, shut the door, and went off walking.

<u>And then what?</u>

I went to get something to eat, and after eating I went to the park to sleep.

The next day I woke up in a strange way. I was asleep and voices, kids' voices, started to wake me up. I opened my eyes and I was surrounded by schoolkids. There was a school opposite the park and these kids, they'd come across during a free period, or maybe it was recess, I don't know, but they were having their snacks there in the park. They were kind of spread out around me, sitting down and eating their *alfajores*, drinking their sodas, chatting.

They paid no attention to me—I guess they probably thought I was a wino who had passed out on the grass. I was woken by the sound of their chatter. Then I did something I was later told conforms with the behavior of a psychopath: I returned to the scene of the crime. According to experts, that's a psychotic act. This time I was much closer, about four blocks away, let's say. The taxi was still there, and there were a couple of police cars too. There were reporters there, the Channel 7 mobile unit, neighbors looking on.

<u>What happened when you saw the taxi? What was that encounter like?</u>

Nothing happened, I don't recall feeling anything when I saw it. [*Melogno reflects.*] When you ask me what I was thinking in those moments, I say "nothing" because, well, it feels like you expect me to recount some sort of strong emotional response, and you have to realize that all this happened while my head was filled with nonsense.

I don't remember how it went, if I stood among the neighbors or whatever. But a reporter came up and asked if I'd heard anything, if I was from the area, if I'd seen anything of what went down.

<u>You were right there, you knew you were responsible for what happened, you had a clear memory?</u>

Yes.

<u>You didn't feel a sense of danger?</u>

No. At no point during that period did I worry about

being caught. I wasn't afraid of the police; I wasn't afraid of going to jail. It wasn't a possibility in the moment.

<u>What did you say in response to the reporter's questions?</u>

I told them I didn't see anything, and that I wasn't from the area.

<u>And why did you go back?</u>

Because I was nearby, only four blocks away.

<u>Was that the only time you returned to the scene of a crime?</u>

Yes.

<u>Why didn't you do it again?</u>

[*Melogno pauses to think.*] Hmmm . . . I mustn't have found anything of interest there . . . does that make sense? No, I guess it doesn't. [*laughter*]

(. . .)

<u>How did you spend the following days leading up to the third killing?</u>

The following days passed more or less in the same way. Movies, walking, wandering.

<u>And inside?</u>

Calm inside. I remember it all as very calm. Every afternoon spent in a cinema, seeing the same film four times. It's like sitting on a sofa all day, listening to the same song play over and over and over, for hours, and you don't even care. Because you're not there, in a certain sense you're not even there.

<u>At one point the newspapers reported that someone</u>

had called the 42nd Precinct to say that they were going to
keep on killing. Was that you?

No. I didn't do those sorts of things. I wasn't following
the case, I didn't check the newspapers to see if they were
running any stories about me, nothing like that.

And when this impulse appeared for a second time, did
you think about it critically at all?

After the first murder, the others happened because of
inertia. From the time of the first murder, the impulse to
kill never went away. I didn't experience it as suffering, or
feel bad about it at all. It was something natural, something
that was just there. There was no anxiety in any of this,
none at all. It was a matter of standing there watching time
go by in my own little world and suddenly I'd feel it in my
body: "The next one."

When you say "my own little world," what do you mean?

My own little world was imagining things. The films
I told you about, the comics, or other things like . . . for
example, in my head I played out the same thing thou-
sands of times: a battle plan for the Spanish Armada
to invade Japan. I'd figure out tactics for both sides, the
Spanish and the Japanese, how they would attack and
defend, how many archers, defenses, ships, cannons, et
cetera, there were on each side. I'd go over the terrain,
all the possible offensive and defensive positions, all that
sort of stuff.

Could you describe the bodily sensation accompanied

with that phrase "the next one"? Something you can recall
about when that feeling came over you?

That's one of the things that has been most difficult for
me to describe. I don't recall hearing voices, but I do remember a feeling, a need inside.

Sometimes . . . for example, you might see a plate with
food on it and seeing it makes you hungry. This was the
opposite. It was something inside: at noon, your stomach
rumbles, you feel something. What is it? Hunger. Although
you haven't seen any food, your body demands food. That's
how it was for me. A physical sensation. I don't know how
else to describe it. Hunger is just an example. The feeling
was different, but it was a bodily sensation of the same sort.
Sometimes I'd spend two or three hours on the corner,
watching cars go by, and suddenly I'd get the feeling: "the
next one." Without seeing it. "The next one." It was like a
premonition. Some of the experts determined that this was
similar to hearing voices. Have you heard the whole story
behind Son of Sam?

Yes.

Well, someone told me about it and you know what?
I just can't understand how a dog could talk to someone. I
just don't get it.

It was a demon, speaking to him through a dog.

Of course. What a complete load of nonsense. Sometimes things are very simple. The legend is one thing, what's
said about a person, but sometimes it's much simpler. In my

case, I never heard voices. I don't remember the feeling as a hallucination, but as something in my body. But by the same token, when I say I could sense spirits in my house as a child, the psychiatrists are quick to say, "There you go, you were having a certain type of hallucination." What was normal or common for me was explained in a more hallucinatory way by the experts.

Speaking of which, after the second killing, I spent a whole day walking around Mataderos, lost in my world. And in the street, I bumped into someone who worked with my old man. She was a woman from Uruguay, a very large woman, with a big bottom, and she was always very curt with me. I'd known her since I was a kid.

<u>Was it the same woman from Uruguay who brought the healer to bless your store?</u>

Yes, that's her. She was a very robust woman, very imposing in a physical sense, and then when I bumped into her on the street . . . She looked strange at first, it was like I was seeing her differently. And then I realized: it was as if she had shrunk. She seemed much smaller, physically. Or maybe I had changed. Maybe I felt bigger, or stronger. In terms of size, in terms of strength, in terms of . . . power. This is an important detail. This sense of largeness was very powerful—what I mean is, for me to be able to remember it so well, it must have been very powerful. Especially with regards to that woman, who was someone you might say I was not necessarily afraid of, but who had been very harsh toward me, someone with a nasty character. And then I saw her as if from above, and it was like, "Things are different now."

It's not like I felt bigger or stronger in front of someone who knew what I'd done and was therefore afraid of me. She had no idea what I had done. There was no change in the other, in the way other people viewed me. For that Uruguayan woman, I was still the same person. But now I felt different when someone looked at me. Something inside me had changed. I'm not sure if I'm making myself clear.

I've had many cellmates, kids who killed people, more often than not while robbing them. And for a person who's killed there's always a certain degree of release that comes from death. Because death transforms them. The power they held in that moment transforms them. Death is crossing a threshold, a threshold of social boundaries. I believe that when someone realizes that everything they've been told about social boundaries doesn't exist, that realization is also the crossing of another threshold.

After those acts there was a transcendental change. Those deaths signified a change, an evolution. The change is imperceptible in the moment. It's like they say in that movie with Keanu Reeves, the one where the orb comes and destroys everything. "Only at the precipice do we evolve."

11

The third man didn't die while you were still in the car—he was taken to a hospital and he died there. Did he seem dead to you when you left him, or were there any signs of life? Could you describe it?

No. None of the people I shot moved afterward. You couldn't see the wound—a .22 caliber makes a very small hole—you couldn't see it through his hair. I'd make sure and see how the shot came out. For example, I'd see if there was blood coming out of their ears. More than anything, this was to make sure what I'd done was irreversible, that there was no turning back. It had to be obvious that the person was never going to recover.

Smoking a couple of cigarettes . . . that was a way of keeping them company, of making sure that the person was dead. I knew, I could feel without seeing, that the driver had slumped over in the front seat, and I was sitting behind him and smoking.

Here it says they found the car with a body inside at 2:00 a.m. on Monday the 27th. What time would the murder have occurred?

Let's say eleven at night. All the deaths occurred before midnight. It was beginning to heat up in the evenings.

Do you remember if you went to your house at any time across those days? Did you shower, change your clothes?

I don't remember, but it's more than likely. I took the drivers' documents and kept them at home. So the answer is yes. I don't remember it, but obviously I went home.

Where did you take that third taxi from?

From Flores. It would have been about twenty blocks from Flores to Mataderos. The corner I gave as my destination turned out to be a dark alleyway. Afterward it was all the same.

A significant detail from that murder was that I can recall going to eat afterward, and the cutlery was sticking to my hands because of the victim's blood.

How did that happen?

I was eating at Dos Hermanos, which as it turns out was only a block and a half away from where I left the car. I sat down to eat and I noticed that the cutlery was sticking to my hands. The first thing that came to my mind was, "Shit, what's happened, I've been magnetized." I looked again, and that wasn't it: there was blood on my hands. The blood was making the cutlery stick to my hands. Shit. I looked at my pants. Bloodstains everywhere. My jacket: more blood-stains. Nothing too extreme, but obvious bloodstains.

So what did you do?

Nothing. I kept eating.

But why did you think you'd been magnetized?

Well, because things were sticking to my hands and I didn't know why. And because those things were metal, I thought that perhaps I was magnetic. The first logical thought was, "The cutlery is made of metal, and if metal is sticking to me . . . then I must be magnetic."

Do you remember if anyone else noticed that you were covered in blood?

No one noticed. And let me tell you something else. I used to go and eat at Dos Hermanos, or at the Carlos Gardel, which was across the road. The Dos Hermanos at that time was a taxi drivers' bar, which is to say that I was eating there along with all the other cabdrivers with their taxis parked outside, and they were shooting the shit, having a drink, whatever. By the second or third killing in Mata-deros, they were already forming a posse to track me down and hang me.

They mentioned that in the papers.

So they were right in front of me, talking about hunting me down and hanging me.

Did you know they were looking for you?

Umm . . . yes. In a strange way, yes. But at the same time, I couldn't give three fucks about anything happening around me.

So it was all about you.

It was all about me.

Did you eat the same thing [*suprema napolitana* and fries] every day, or only when you had killed?

When I was arrested, I was very skinny, I'd lost a lot of weight. I walked a lot and I ate very little. Sometimes just a bit of bread, or I'd go to a pastry shop and buy one of those little *alfajor* cakes. They were very cheap. I'd sit down in a plaza and eat.

So you only ate *suprema napolitana* and fries when you'd killed someone?

That's right. I have no recollection of the moment of death, but I remember the sense of satisfaction afterward, of going and eating the *suprema* with fries and a chocolate mousse for dessert. I remember how good it tasted.

Now, in hindsight, I'd say it was kind of like a celebration.

What were you celebrating? That something important had happened?

That anything at all had happened, you could say.

12

Do you remember anything in particular from the final incident? The one that took place on the corners of Basualdo and Tapalqué.

It's really strange around there. No, that one went down the same as the others. The driver looked at the meter, turned around to charge me, and then I shot him and turned off the engine.

If you shot the drivers at the moment they turned around to charge you, when did you take the gun out?

When I got into the cab, I'd put the leather bag next to my thigh, and then I'd get it out during the trip. By the time we arrived at the destination I already had the gun in my hand.

Did you close your eyes then as well?

Yes. I think so. I'm not sure, actually.

<u>If you had your eyes closed, how did you manage to hit
your target on four different occasions?</u>

I told you I had my eyes closed, but the truth is I have
no memory of the moment I pulled the trigger. I can remember the sound of the gunshot inside the car, and then
the guy slumped over. That's all I have in my head.

From that occasion, I can remember that the diesel engine was making a horrible noise, and I switched it off because it was too loud. I saw a light go on outside a house a
few meters away. I figured they must have seen me, and if
they had a phone, they'd already be calling the police. All
the same I stayed there for a while, smoking my cigarette.
Nothing happened. Then I got out of the car and wandered
through the streets until I found my way to Dos Hermanos.

I walked for a few blocks and then I went down a dead
end. Spring was about to begin, so it wasn't cold. There were
people out on the sidewalks, even though it was late. I came
out of the alley and then something incredible happened: a
taxi came up from behind and pulled up in front of me. An
armed man got out of the taxi and pointed his gun at me,
telling me to stop. I went to get my pistol out of the purse
but before I could, the other guy raised his weapon and
fired at me. I recall perfectly—at this stage I no longer have
the memory, but I know that at the time I could remember
it—the click of the hammer on the revolver . . . and then,
nothing. No shot, no bullet. I watched him freeze, staring

at the revolver in confusion. Then I got my gun out and pointed it at him. The guy said "I'm not a cop" and I told him to get back in the car and leave. He threw the gun into the back seat, got in, and the taxi took off.

How far was this from the scene of the crime?

Four or five blocks. Everyone was looking at me. I had a military ID card, so I got it out and held it up: "Argentine Army, nothing to see here!" Everyone stayed calm. No one understood the first thing about what was going on, but seeing as there was a military ID card in play, no one did anything, so I left. I walked for a few more blocks until I arrived at the restaurant. I ate there, same as always.

Where did you get that military ID from?

They had let me out of military service but they hadn't fully discharged me, because I still had a case pending. Even though they let me go, every now and again I still wore the uniform, and I had an ID card that said "Private Ricardo Melogno, 1962 Class, is under active duty in the Engineering Detail of Villa Martelli under the direction of the chief command of the Army." During the military dictatorship, having a piece of paper like that was a real jackpot. I'd covered mine in plastic to protect it.

Why didn't you kill that last guy who confronted you? I mean, the guy actually pulled the trigger on you . . .

Yeah, OK, but, umm . . . well, I guess there were people there watching. And anyway, at the time I had a different answer to that question. It wasn't his fate to die there.

<u>After you ate, what did you do?</u>
I went to sleep in the park.
<u>With that last act, was it all over?</u>
It was all over, yes.
<u>Why was it all over?</u>
This is kind of what confuses the psychiatrists. It was an explosion that lasted a few days, that began without any apparent cause and finished on its own, too. It ended as quickly as it began.

I've never been able to explain it: not why it started, or why it ended. The closest I could get is to say that my desire to do it, my impulse went away.

(. . .)

At one point, to talk about this, to sketch out the idea, I used the phrase, "If I felt like eating, I ate, if I felt like sleeping, I slept, and if I felt like killing, I killed." A stupid thing to say that did me no favors in court. But when I talk about "feeling like it" I don't mean it the way you might say "I feel like going to the theatre." If you feel sleepy it's not that you feel like sleeping: you actually *start* falling asleep. That's how it is if you're sitting, lying down, standing up. You fall asleep, or you go into a daze. It's not like you're trying to fall asleep; sleep comes, no matter where you are. It was the same thing for me—it's not like I felt like going out and killing people. It was something natural that happened to me, that flowed through me. Let's say you're tired, you're up writing and you get tired and then you fall asleep. That's something that just *happens*, you can't control it. You go into a daze and you end up falling asleep. It's something that happened by itself, it wasn't something I hoped for or thought about or wanted. It just came. I had no sense of control over the acts.

<u>If you hadn't been arrested, do you think you would have gone on killing?</u>

I can't speculate on what might have happened. It might have kept happening, it might have gotten worse, or maybe it never would have happened again. I can't speculate because they picked me up in the afternoon and by the evening I was in a cell in a straitjacket and they gave me a shot to send me to sleep. From then on it was over twenty years of injections and psychiatric medication in industrial quantities.

<u>Did you understand that the murders had taken place in the real world?</u>

The way I acted back then indicates that to a certain extent, I was aware that the deaths had occurred. Taking the documents, making a shrine for protection, wandering around Mataderos even though I knew they were after me. External factors. But there was no internal thought where I said, "Fuck, what kind of a shit storm have I made for myself now" or anything like that. It was more like, ummm . . . from that time I don't even have any recollection of thinking along those lines after killing. From the acts themselves you can see that nothing existed for me.

13

Afterward, I rented a little room in a family hotel in Mataderos. Actually, the night that I killed for the last time, I slept in the park as well. But the next day I put on my uniform, went to the hotel, and spent a few days living with a roof over my head. I remember the feeling of lying down in a bed with proper sheets and sleeping, calm and relaxed, in the sense that I didn't have to worry about what was happening around me. I had an impulse to go there. I was so tired. I slept through the whole first day in the hotel without waking up. I slept like the dead. The other days weren't as extreme as that, but I spent them sleeping as well.

Then I went back to the streets, but by then I was already—I don't know if I'd say peaceful, but I was . . . locked back in to a "normal" rhythm of life, you could say.

<u>During those days, did you go back to the warehouse at all?</u>

No. I didn't go back there while I was at the hotel, because I didn't need to. But afterward, when I was back on the streets, I started using the warehouse again. I'd head back there from time to time.

A few days went by like that, until my father went to the warehouse one day to look for something, and by chance stumbled across the taxi drivers' documents. He was looking for something else, but that's what he found. I don't know how that all happened. I wasn't there, obviously.

<u>Were the documents hidden?</u>

No, they weren't hidden. They were in a corner of the warehouse; they were on a kind of altar that I'd half-covered.

<u>The newspapers never mentioned the altar.</u>

That's because my father took the altar down when he found it. It's not mentioned in the papers but it does feature in the court transcripts, because I brought it up myself. I was asked why I kept those things that could incriminate me, and that's when I explained that I had a little altar with the photos of my victims, which was like a defense against their souls. The drivers always had a little bag with all their things inside it, so I would take that, and eventually I'd keep the documents and throw the rest away.

<u>Did you place the documents on the altar from the very first murder?</u>

Yes.

<u>What was the altar made of?</u>

It was a nook where there was a little shelf, and that's where I put the documents. I just propped them up side by side against the wall. Nothing very elaborate.

<u>Did you sit there and look at them? How did that work?</u>

No, nothing like that. I didn't pray at the altar or light candles, no rituals. I just kept the documents there. After every incident I took the driver's documents and left them there on the altar. There was nothing religious about it, it was more for protection. It was like a way of keeping the souls present. They were there, that's all. And that's why they were found. If they had been more important to me in ritual terms, I'd have hidden them better. It wasn't a religious thing. There was no higher being directing my actions, no calling of any kind.

<u>And what did your father do when he found the documents?</u>

He waited for me. He knew that sooner or later I'd turn up at the warehouse. When I arrived, he told me he wanted to speak to me in his office. My brother was there too. Everything was cool. I went into the office, and left my bag resting on a machine. My father came from behind me, grabbed the bag, and because of the weight he realized the gun was inside it. Then they began to talk to me, to tell me what had happened. They told me they were going to help me flee the country, and they took me to my brother's house. We had dinner, we went to bed, and the next day my brother left early and my father stayed in the house with me. We had breakfast. Meanwhile my brother had gone to meet with the judge and turn me in.

<u>What did you think about the possibility of fleeing the country?</u>

Nothing. That night I lay down on the mattress and I slept like a brick. The next day I could have escaped. My brother went to turn me in, and at that same time my father went to buy bread. If I'd thought about escaping, I could have slipped away right then.

At one point my father said, "They've come to take you away now." I opened the door and there were two policemen pointing guns at me. A man in a suit walked in and said, "How are you, Ricardo? I'm Judge Miguel Ángel Caminos, and from this moment on you are under my protection, no one is going to hurt you." "OK," is all I said. The second guy to walk into the house was a forensic doctor. He shook my hand and at the same time grabbed my wrist to take my pulse, then straightaway they put me in a Falcon and took me off to the courthouse.

<u>Your brother uttered the phrase "clear his name" when he entered the judge's office, according to the newspapers.</u>

I think that must have been because of the gun. My old man had two guns, a .32 caliber revolver and the pistol, a .22 caliber Bersa. In his judicial statement, my father said that

I had stolen his pistol. But I never stole it, he gave it to me. He was protecting himself a little from everything that was coming down on him. I understood that; it seemed like a pretty logical reaction.

Did anyone hide the gun in the roof? In the newspapers it was said that the gun was hidden in a box inside a water tank in the warehouse roof.

No. I never kept the gun there. But I did used to go up to the rooftop terrace and spend time there, so maybe someone saw me there and that's what they thought.

So another thing you did when you went to the warehouse was go up to the rooftop?

Yes, looking for isolation. It was a place where I could be in my own world, where I could talk calmly without worrying about anyone in the street seeing me talk or gesticulate to myself. I could spend a whole afternoon doing that. I had been doing that since I was a kid. Rooftops are quiet places. No one bothers you there.

When did your father give you the pistol?

When I got out of military service and he set up the business for me. He gave it to me just in case. For self-defense, you might say.

If your father had never given you the gun, if you'd never had access to a weapon, what do you think would have happened?

I think that sooner or later something would have happened. The gun wasn't the problem.

<u>Do you remember anything from the moment when
your father gave you the gun? Was it an important moment
for you?</u>

No, there was nothing special about it—it was for
safety, just in case, for the business. I saw no special power
in the weapon. Don't forget, I'd just come from shooting
FAL and FAP assault rifles, heavy weaponry.

I might as well tell you: when my father gave me the pistol, I began to use it as a pillow. Locked, loaded, and with
the safety off.

<u>Why?</u>

For the same reason I used to sleep with a knife under
my pillow.

<u>Could you still feel the presence of spirits?</u>

Yes. That's not something that you get away from. It's
not like taking off a T-shirt and putting on a different one.

<u>When did you stop feeling the presence of spirits?</u>

That happened gradually over the years, when I was in
jail, because of the environment I was in. By then my real
surroundings were more frightening than anything I could
possibly imagine. If you're afraid of spirits and all of a sudden you have to sleep in a room full of scorpions, first you
should be scared of the scorpions.

14

The same night they arrested me, I was sent directly to the Caseros Prison. I was processed, they explained a few things to me, and then all of a sudden they threw me to the ground, put a straitjacket on me, and gave me my first injection. They gave me tranquilizers, and I spent nearly a whole week asleep. The doctors came and checked on me—they'd open my eyes and if they saw I was half-awake, bam, they'd give me another injection. To eat, two men came to my cell, took me out of the straitjacket, and gave me some food. I was allowed to go to the toilet with the two guys there in front of me, and then it was straight back to bed to sleep some more. I recovered twenty days later. That's the sleep cure, and then you have to recover from the cure itself. Get all of those chemicals out of you. Which is to say: I had just come from being outside of space and time, and here was another period that was completely blank for me.

When I came out of the sleep cure, I was sent to the eighth floor. Caseros was a huge building, twenty stories high. The eighth floor was kind of middle-class. It wasn't a complete mess, but it wasn't good either. From the fourth floor down, you had the old guys with money. They had bigger cells, other comforts. From the tenth floor up, it was a real ghetto, no other word for it. It got worse the higher up you went. The eighth floor was a unit for big dogs, for reoffenders. They sent me there to break me.

<u>Break you how?</u>

Well, they turn you over to the lifers.

<u>So that they could fuck you in the ass?</u>

Yes, that's one of the ways they could ruin your life. That was very common. The thing is I was looking at a life sentence, so their idea was that it would best for me to be killed off as soon as possible, or for me to go ahead and kill myself.

But I got lucky, because the lifers liked me. First of all, it was because of my case, because I didn't care about anything, four murders, life in prison. Second of all, it was my behavior—it was kind of obvious that I wasn't going to cause any conflicts. And also there was simple curiosity, from what had been in the papers, on the radio, and on TV.

(. . .)

A few months into my time in jail, I got extremely depressed, I felt like killing myself.

<u>Why?</u>

Boredom. It's so boring being in a cell that's two by one

meters for twenty-four hours a day. That's boredom on a
horrific, desperate level. I looked terrible. By the way, this is
a very typical phase for an inmate. And then this thief came
along, an old-timer with a shiv made from the sharpened
handle of a spoon, and he said something that stuck with
me: "Look, man, from here you've got two choices: if you
want to kill yourself, do it right. Go up to the bars, grab a
guard and stick him. You take his key, then go to the next
door and kill the guards there. And you just keep going
till they kill you or you get away. If they kill you, you'll be
left with a rep for being a crazy motherfucker who killed a
couple of pigs. The other option? Learn to live here, learn to
do time. Learn to listen, to keep quiet."

(. . .)

<u>In your case, what was the sequence of jails you were
sent to?</u>

I spent five years in regular jail, between Caseros and
Devoto, with a six-month stretch in Melchor Romero,
the last month of which I was officially listed as "missing."
In 1987 I was given Article 34 [insanity] and they sent me to
Unit 20 at the Borda Hospital. I was in Unit 20 from 1987
until the fire in 2011, when they closed it and transferred
us here [psychiatric hospital of the Ezeiza Penitentiary
Complex].

In Caseros we had individual cells. Come what may, you
could live your own life a little. They put me on meds there.
In terms of volume, it was much less than in Unit 20, and

besides, they never checked if you actually took them or not. You could keep the pills and trade them for things; it was like having money. Every morning they gave you medication and it was like going to a bank teller to take out cash. That was very helpful to me.

In Devoto there were communal cellblocks. There were over a hundred of us but only fifty stretcher-beds. In the solitary confinement blocks, you couldn't stand up because there wasn't enough room, and you couldn't lie down either. It was like a little nook, but very uncomfortable. The door was made of metal sheeting with a little opening where they could throw water in, so that you wouldn't lie down or fall asleep. What I most remember about Devoto is the smell. A mixture of odors, a rancid stench. We cooked on kerosene stoves. The smell of food and kerosene, the noise, twenty different people, each with their own radio, trying to drown out the noise coming from everyone else's. In winter they closed the windows because of the cold and it was like drowning; the air was sucked out of you. People slept during the day and wandered around at night. In Devoto I learned to sleep dressed and with my shoes on, ready to spring up at the slightest movement. Because there was always someone awake, prowling around. They could come and try to rob you, or get you back for something you had done to them. So you had to adapt: you'd be sleeping and all of a sudden you'd feel a shadow stop in front of you and bam! You'd wake up. This instinct takes control of you.

The place is fucked up. No matter how calm and settled things seem, you live with a sixth sense for waiting for the next threat to come. Because you know that sooner or later, things are going to blow up. It's like paranoia, but it's also a survival instinct.

(. . .)

How did you end up "missing" in Melchor Romero?

They sent me there to have some tests done, and while I was there I had to fight another inmate, not another crazy person but a normal inmate who was kind of hiding out there. He was the warden's snitch, and I stabbed him a few times but I didn't kill him. The warden didn't like that, and as a punishment I spent thirty days staked out on a bed frame. My arms and legs spread, my ankles and wrists cuffed to the bed. They gave me insulin shocks: they were using insulin in the place of electroshocks. I don't know what the exact reaction is, but in any case, you end up in a bad way, really fucked up. This takes place in a solitary cell that has a door with a tiny peephole and a sign that says BIOLOGY. When I arrived, I noticed something weird with that door. We were on the way to the exercise yard. When they took us out, we'd walk right past it, and I noticed that the crazy inmates avoided the door, they'd run past it if they had to, as if they were afraid of it. And then I found out why they were afraid.

They told my father I wasn't there anymore, that I'd been transferred. He spent a month searching for me until he came back with a federal judge—by this stage I had been declared missing—and he pulled me out of there. I was destroyed, I could barely move.

They used to call Melchor Romero the House of Terror. It was a big old mansion like in *The Addams Family*, in the middle of the countryside. It was surrounded by grass and a double fence with a guard on each corner. The guards were armed with a Mauser, the short Mauser that only shoots one shot. It was a weapon from the First World War, more or less. The guards themselves were peasants from the area—they lived on rabbits they hunted. They only needed one shot to bring you down.

The day I arrived, there was a nurse in the intake room seeing to an inmate whose ear was injured. The guy had fallen asleep and a rat had eaten half his ear.

<u>How come he didn't wake up, if a rat was chewing on his ear?</u>

The thing is, rats have a kind of anesthetic in their saliva, and while they're chewing on you, you don't feel a thing.

15

Very few people know about my history with religion. Well, those who've known me a long time know it all, but apart from that I keep quiet about the whole thing. I'm used to talking with psychiatrists and psychologists who see my beliefs as "strange religious ideations." It's just another thing they use to classify me, but still they classify me wrong. That's why I try not to talk about it too much. Many of the employees of the Federal Penitentiary Service are Christians—most of them are evangelicals. So, when it comes to religion, they're very firm about rejecting anything that's not Christianity. Sometimes the evangelicals get to a terrifying level of evangelism. Those people are scary. Truly scary.

Religion here in prison? In the beginning I realized it could be used as a defense, and I fooled around with it for a long time. It started out as a prison joke. In Caseros, I was the crazy kid, the joker of the cellblock. One day another inmate came up to me with a tiny coffin, a pretty little thing, painted black. The guy had a hobby of making little boats out of balsa wood. He came up to me with this coffin and said, "Look what I made for you, blah blah blah, this, that, the other thing . . . you wouldn't have a pill, would you?" That's what we call a "prison rope": "You're such a great guy, so smart, you're the best, blah blah blah . . . you wouldn't have some tomato sauce to cook with, would you?" It's a classic way to get ahold of things. And, well, I ended up with the coffin in my cell and I said to myself, "I'm going to put a doll in it." So, I made a little doll and put it in the coffin.

What did you make the doll out of?

Bread crumbs, toilet paper, and blood.

Whose blood?

Mine. I asked the guy to make me three more coffins, and in each of them I put a little doll with the name of one of my victims. In the cell there was a kind of metal shelf, so I put them all up there and made an altar. And that's how I came up with something that helped protect me. I got lucky stumbling across these things, you know, like when you think school is just a pain in the ass and then all of a sudden, the moment comes where you think, "Fuck, all that shit I learned and couldn't care less about, now it's become useful." If I, the evil maniac, make a little doll, execute it, and hang it from the bars on the cell, then the doll protects me. At the very least, it scares or worries any guy who sees me do it. In Santería, altars and objects are often arranged so that they protect a doorway. Even people with garden gnomes know this. If you look, you'll see garden gnomes are always guarding doors.

It's survival.

Over time, this took off. First it was a couple of inmates who came along with little bits of paper: "Ricardo, can I leave this with your things, in exchange for a little favor?" One day we were in the prison yard at Caseros, the big yard. There were some windows that looked out onto the street, and we'd made some holes in the windows so you could pop your head out and speak with visitors, out there in the street. Someone said, "*Che*, a guy down there is asking for you," so I went down and there was another inmate, one who had left a little bit of paper in my cell and had then been released. He'd come to thank me, as if that was part of the reason he'd got out. Two hours later, even the guards were leaving little papers on my altar.

There's a lot of superstition in prison. One guy gets released, and straightaway another guy wants to sleep in the bed the other guy just left behind. Because that guy got out.

<u>What were the favors the guards asked for?</u>

Mostly they had to do with love or relationships, and lots of favors relating to work: transfers, things like that. At that time the prison guards were brutish people, from the interior of the country. There was a joke going around that said that to recruit guards, the Penitentiary Service went out to the mountains in the Chaco, laid ten pairs of boots at the foot of a tree, and shook it. Those who fell into the boots became officers, and those who didn't, NCOs.

Perhaps I didn't have that evil streak, or all that prison knowledge, but my cellmates certainly did. "Oh, the guards don't go into the maniac's cell, they're afraid," they'd say. "Let's leave our things in here." And the guys began to buy into that too, because it served them as well.

In the end there was a consensus that I truly was making these things happen. The inmates, and even the guards, too, began to avoid coming into my cell. It was all nonsense, but during shakedowns they went over my altar without touching a thing. The guards had their own mean streak with each other. They'd always send the dumbest one to shake down my cell: "Go to the maniac's cell. Touch his things and your hands will fall off." That's how the legend really took off: "Maniac, I had to touch your things, it's my job, I did it respectfully, I didn't break anything."

I have this thing where . . . people say that when I get angry I transform, the look on my face changes, my whole way of being changes. Mystics say I have a force that surrounds me, and they can see it.

Because they're mystics?

Because they're believers. Christians, or believers in some other faith. Believers I've come across.

(. . .)

Once, a group of guys got together and began to prepare an escape. They had a gun smuggled in, a small .25 caliber pistol with ammunition, as well as a switchblade, and they were waiting for a few more things to arrive. During a routine inspection the bullets were discovered. The guards got nervous, and they began to search through the whole unit looking for the gun. They never found the gun, but they found the switchblade in my cell. There were five of us in the cell, and they put a lot of physical pressure on us during the interrogation, lots of abuse. When it was my turn, I decided on the fly to take responsibility for the switchblade. I said it was mine. They asked me why I had it and I said it was for religious use. "I use it on Fridays, to kill cats. In my religion we make blood sacrifices." Besides all that, it wasn't a shiv made in prison, it was a real switchblade brought from the outside. It's very difficult to get a thing like that through security, so they asked me how I got it. "One of the guards got it for me. He was having trouble with his wife, and I did some couples therapy for him. In exchange I asked for the knife, because I needed it for the ceremony." "What's the guard's name?" "I'm no snitch, why would I tell you his name?" And so they confiscated the switchblade, but that was the end of the matter.

At that moment, when I made that declaration about the cats and the sacrifices, it was to cover up something bigger, so the guards would leave it there and not dig any deeper. But there were consequences: the statement was passed up the chain and it ended up in my file. From then on, years would go by and forensic specialists would meet with me and say things like "How's it going, Melogno, how's the cat hunting going? Any sacrifices lately? Aren't your buddies worried you'll run out of cats one day?" They've never forgotten about that.

(. . .)

Things went along like that until this one time, when I must have been thirty-two or thirty-three years old, and I had been sent to solitary in Unit 20. I had a massive religious experience there, and I realized that there really was something inside me, in a religious sense. It was something natural, that no one else had taught me.

<u>Like what, for example?</u>

Certain prayers that were deeply ingrained inside me. Or rituals, certain things that I would do at a given time. Little dolls, things that I would make and that worked. On a functional level, the defenses I made worked very well in those spaces. So then the big question is *why* do they work?

I realized that there were things inside me that led me to religion. Things like . . . well, they were already there. My mother never did voodoo rituals, but I knew how to make voodoo dolls. There were things that were already there inside me. It was a defense that worked . . . and I said to myself, "Shit, how did I do that? Where did I get that from?" It wasn't something I'd learned.

I believe that with every reincarnation the soul takes a

path that is either purifying, or initiatory. I believe that my religious knowledge does not come from this life. I figure my life comes from beforehand, it's a path I've been forging from previous lives, and that the soul preserves any knowledge you acquire. Some things are natural. My understanding, or my madness, makes me believe this.

So, at thirty-two or thirty-three years old, locked away in solitary in Unit 20, I said to myself, "I've been fooling and messing around with this stuff for so long. Either I embrace it, accept it and live it seriously, or I let it go." What I mean is it seemed like what I'd been doing up to that point was just deceiving myself through faith and deceiving faith itself. I decided to respect faith and take it seriously.

Religion isn't about a person who has some kind of existential desire. It's something you already have, something you carry inside you from before. Not because you search for it, but because you've already found it.

16

When I was twenty-five, twenty-six years old, I was declared mentally insane, not responsible for my actions. Then I was interned in Unit 20, the penitentiary unit of the José Tiburcio Borda psychiatric hospital. There, no matter what you were committed for, the protocol was that you'd have three injections a day (morning, noon, and night) for fifteen days. They called it "Cocktail No. 20" and it was a pretty heavy mix of psychiatric medications. After those fifteen days had passed—that's forty-five injections in a row—they gave you ten days to come down, and then twenty more to observe you to see how you reacted and determine which wing they'd put you in. This whole time you were naked in a room one and a half meters by two meters, and your bed was just a concrete slab. It was like being in solitary, except your ass was covered in abscesses from all the needles.

Compared to normal jail, Unit 20 was calmer, because

so many people were on medication. Many of them weren't even convicted criminals, they were sick people from the "normal" part of Borda, and they'd been sent over to us as punishment. They were people who were out of control: alcoholics, drug addicts, people who caused trouble and couldn't get by in Borda. They all had psychiatric illnesses. But it wasn't quite like normal jail; it wasn't like being in the can.

I had come from Devoto, from a proper cellblock where you spent your whole day waiting for the shit to hit the fan. So in comparison, Unit 20 seemed a little boring. There was no radio, no TV. There was an old tube television in the back. There was no way of telling what time it was. If they saw you trying to exercise, they'd give you an injection; they didn't like you moving around too much. You weren't allowed a watch, and barely anyone had a radio. You kind of oriented yourself around meal times: "I'm hungry," you'd say to yourself. "It must be nearly lunch time." On the other hand, everything was way calmer, so you could let your guard down a bit. People took siestas in the afternoon.

I was already pretty medicated. In Caseros and Devoto they gave me pills, but they never checked if I took them or not. In Unit 20 you had to take them no matter what; there was a nurse with a shoehorn that he used to check your mouth and make sure you swallowed them. From that moment on, and for the next twenty years, I was given anti-psychotics of all kinds in industrial quantities.

Unit 20 was an aberration. At the time, it was the prison unit with the most complaints for mistreatment in the country. Every year there were two or three deaths from overmedication, often from injections. You arrived there and for fifteen days they'd pump you full of Cocktail No. 20, and there were lots of people who couldn't take it, their hearts couldn't handle it and they died. And nobody gave a shit. Bah, sometimes a patient would die on one of the nurses and then they weren't allowed to give injections anymore, so they couldn't work. But generally speaking, nothing mattered to anyone. An inmate would die because their body couldn't stand the chemical impact and they'd say it was "natural causes." Many crazy people hanged themselves too. There were many curious cases of hangings, where the inmate had been beaten to a pulp just the day before, the day before they hanged themselves. That was called "natural causes" too. Natural in the sense that it's natural to die when someone hangs you.

They came in and closed Unit 20—after many years—because of all the mistreatment, the beatings, and the suspicious deaths. And because it had become like a vault. Any judge who had a psychiatric patient who was proving difficult would toss them in Unit 20 and forget about them. Most of them were from other provinces, so that was part of it too. In their own provinces the courts had nowhere to dump a guy, so they sent him to Unit 20. Then they get cut off from their families, every tie is severed and they're there alone, they're crazy, they know no one. They have no way of causing trouble for the jurisdictions that sent them there. Unit 20 was like a vault full of people you could just lock up and forget about.

17

Of the astronomical quantities of psychiatric medications that were administered to me throughout my years in Unit 20, the worst of all was haloperidol.

Haloperidol makes everything contract. Your tongue rolls to one side, your jaw tightens. For me the effect was like being packed in tight on a bus, my legs all stiff. I couldn't lie down; I spent the whole day on my feet, and then my legs would cramp from all the walking. It was the same if I was in solitary, a little cell two by one meter in size. I'd be walking, I'd lie down for five minutes, then bang! I'd be up on my feet like a spring, walking around again. The body does this by itself, you have no control over it at all. You say to yourself, "Fucking hell, I'd love to lie down," and you just can't. It destroys you. You can tell if a nutcase is on haloperidol because he stumbles along like a robot, drooling like the walking dead. You can't follow a movie, you can't think. The worst part is that it destroys your imagination. It kills your creative process. Everything becomes rubbery, monotonous. You turn into an oddball, a zombie.

For many years I was medicated with haloperidol decanoate, an injectable form of the medication that stays in your blood for thirty days and has a progressive effect. They just inject you and forget about it. Sometimes the nurses forgot, or the date to be dosed again slipped by, and then you got the haloperidol comedown, which is a dark, dismal depression. You watch the walls, everything seems dirty, the furniture and everything else feels sticky. You want to kill yourself.

Once I had to spend a month in a hospital outside of Unit 20, detoxing from haloperidol. I remember being in the shower at one point and realizing that I was alive. It's a feeling that I can remember very clearly, very vividly. Being beneath the water, holding on to the walls of the bathroom. I remember looking at my arms, my hands. I could see that my hands were there, holding on to the walls, and I thought, "Son of a bitch, I'm alive, I can't believe it." It was like surfacing again. That feeling of surfacing. I said it again: "I'm alive, son of a bitch." I looked at my hands on the tiles of the bathroom wall and said, "I'm alive." The *feeling* of being alive . . . that moment is something I remember so clearly. It was like I had surfaced, I was there, once more.

(. . .)

I was also really into pills as a recreational thing, Artane mostly. Artane gives you hallucinations, like LSD, but a little different. The way to do it is to stretch out on your bed in the dark, and then all your thoughts are hyperreal. It's quite common to think you're smoking, but there's no cigarette in your hand. People burn their faces trying to light a cigarette that isn't in their mouths. You forget what you're talking about, and you can't sleep. You take about twenty pills, let's say.

<u>All at once?</u>

No, a few at a time. It begins to hit you and your throat tightens and you can't swallow anything. Everything looks blurry. You can't see the hairs on the back of your hand when you're high, and then you know you're coming down when you can see them again. Going to the bathroom on Artane is weird too, because it relaxes your whole body, so it feels pretty strange when you take a shit. Artane is a really strong medication, at least it was at the time. With many medications, once junkies start using them recreationally, they change the formula. Artane is a medication for Parkinson's disease, it's vasodilatory. It stops you from shaking and allows for more blood to flow to the brain, which I figure must be what makes the trip so strong.

<u>Is it fucked up at any point? Is there a bad moment to the trip?</u>

The comedown. Because you've been on a two-day bender, you want to sleep but you can't. You can drink milk to shorten the comedown, but because you can't eat, you have this strange, disgusting feeling in your stomach, a feeling of unease. When I was around thirty, I contracted two forms of hepatitis, and my liver is pretty touchy now. So I stopped taking pills. The comedown, more so than the assault on the liver, had already become unbearable.

(. . .)

Klonopin is another jailhouse drug, but a shitty drug, the worst jailhouse drug there is. Klonopin has the same basic makeup as Rohypnol, but it's a clinical drug for epilepsy, while Rohypnol is a psychiatric drug. Rohypnol is the type of pill you take and you have no idea what you've done to yourself, you don't remember a thing. You go into the cellblock's refrigerator and you eat everyone else's food, nothing matters to you, you'll say anything to anyone, and then the next day you have to pay for all the trouble you've caused. Klonopin is the same thing. The trip is very similar. The next day you wake up feeling aggressive, terrible, and you feel like smashing in the face of anyone who speaks to you. If Klonopin gets around a cellblock, it means there'll be trouble, inevitably.

There was a kind of famous massacre at the prison in Villa Devoto because of Klonopin. Two hundred pills found their way in there. They came in at midday, and by 3:00 p.m. the first fight had broken out. We caught sight of a guy walking around all nervous with socks over his hands. We knew that trick: underneath the socks he was hiding a shiv. We saw him like that and thought, here comes trouble. At one point he sat down on a bed and began chatting with someone. They were just sitting there talking and suddenly he stabbed the other guy three times. It was summer, the other guy was fat, with a big belly, and he was wearing shorts but they were unbuttoned. Reacting to the stabbing and the surprise of it all, the fat guy tried to scramble away, but his shorts fell down and he couldn't hold on to them. One of the knife thrusts hit near his heart, and you could see the heart beating and little spurts of blood coming out of the wound. The guards saw that brawl go down, put locks on the three doors and then disappeared, leaving us there alone. That's when all the other brawls flared up. To sum up: two days locked up like that, with guys drugged to the eyeballs beating each other up and stabbing each other. There were walkways above with metal bars on them, and the guards just strolled along, even the warden was there, stirring up trouble and making comments, egging us on. On the third day they came in to carry out the dead and the wounded and to restore order. It's pretty simple; they're not idiots. If they'd come in when the first fight broke out, it would have been the whole cellblock against them. A hardcore cellblock, men serving life without parole, all of them on drugs. So what did they do? They let the prisoners murder each other, and once everyone had calmed down, they went in.

(. . .)

At one point I got really into making booze. I became a

real perfectionist about it. I've always been the best brewer of *pajarito* [prison hooch] in every cellblock I've been sent to. I take care with it, I give it time, take it nice and easy. I keep it warm and look after it.

Pajarito is just fermentation. Usually you make it in five-liter jerry cans. Sometimes, if you've got a container that's big enough, you can make it in a twenty-liter jug. But then it's harder to stash, and besides, there's the smell. There's a constant smell of yeast that can give you away, because it's so strong. The smell is like a snitch right there in the cell, and the other thing is you have to be careful it doesn't explode. You have to open it every now and again, because otherwise, the fermentation makes the jug explode, or it seeps out a little. If you know how to look after it, it's delicious. I made *pajarito* that was so good that some old-timers took a sip and said, "Maniac, you must have bought this on the outside, this is champagne." I just showed them the jug and told them nope, I made it right here.

What do you make it from?

Sugar and yeast. That's where the alcohol comes from. If you can keep it at sixty degrees, you can distill alcohol. In the prison library all kinds of strange things would turn up, really old books, from the 1930s, like scrolls almost. Once I found a book that was about old customs and making things—it taught you how to make alcohol, keeping it at sixty degrees, the whole shebang. From this book

I learned how to make a little still, to ferment the alcohol better. It's also where I learned about fermentation times, et cetera, and I began improvising: with potato you make vodka, with rice you make sake, you can make wine out of beetroot, with oranges or apples you can make champagne. It all depends on what fruit you can get. *Pajarito* with potato is the worst, the nastiest, the one that fucks you up the most. It makes a really strong vodka. Well, something like vodka. We're not talking about clear liquor here. It's murky. It comes out white. It's not like you can refine it.

<u>So there are lots of particles floating around in it?</u>

Yeah. And then you have to filter it through a sock.

18

One quality that marks me as a psychopath is my lack of emotions. According to the forensic medical profession, I have all the emotions of a paving stone.

I wasn't raised to have emotions. If you have no knowledge of emotions, or if you're not raised with them, you can't recognize them. You can't understand them.

In Unit 20 I met with a psychologist who had me work on my emotions. She had me work with my father, who was the only person who came to visit me, and she kind of forced me to ask him certain things when he came to see me.

<u>What sort of things?</u>

Well, I was very out of it on medication, it wasn't something I was able to think too deeply about. It was more about actions. For example, my father would come to see me and we would shake hands. The way we related to each other was very distant. So she asked why we never hugged each other. My old man told me he'd been raised that way, I don't know . . . in any case, from those discussions onward we started greeting each other with a hug, and over time the distance between us began to close. We became friendlier with each other. It was a link I never shared with my brothers. My father came to visit me for eleven years, until he got Alzheimer's and he couldn't come anymore. Then he caused a couple of problems and they had to send him to a nursing home. After that he died. That's the only time my brother came, along with my other brother who lives in the United States. They came to tell me my father had died. Apart from that, no one else ever visited me.

<u>What did you talk about during your visits?</u>

He told me news about what was going on outside, his job, we'd talk about how I was doing, things like that. Nothing too complicated either; it was difficult for me to keep up a conversation. They were pumping thirty milligrams of haloperidol into me a day.

(. . .)

My parents separated when I was eight years old—or rather, my father left me with my mother, and he sort of disappeared from the family at that point. He would come by on the weekends and take me and my brothers out. I liked those little outings, but my brother told me he hated them. My old man loved to walk—I think I inherited that from him. He would take us to the Rural, and to other exhibition centers, and we'd walk and walk and walk. My brother told me he hated those afternoons we spent walking. I liked walking, because for better or worse it gave me the mental freedom I needed. I'd go off into my own world and nothing bothered me, but my brother had a much worse time of it.

Did your father ever say to you "Son, your mother and I have separated?" Did you ever have that conversation?

No. We never talked about family. I don't know how my parents met. The other day I was wearing a Nueva Chicago soccer jersey and one of the teachers here said, "Hey, you're from Mataderos, I bet you were born in the Salaberry Hospital." And I had no idea. They never told me those sorts of things.

Your father never told you why they separated?

No, we didn't speak about it. Let me tell you something strange: when they lived together, my parents slept in the same bed, but . . . well, in the few memories I have . . . they slept in separate positions.

In separate beds?

No, in the same bed, a queen-size bed, but they slept at opposite ends, head to toe.

(. . .)

Just so you know how deep my father got into things over time: in 1991 or 1992 I tried to escape from Unit 20. To do this I swallowed twenty-seven razor blades, because the plan was to have myself operated on and then escape from the hospital. My old man, who was a shoemaker, made me a pair of shoes with a whole system of layers underneath with a catch, sewn up tight, and inside it he'd stitched a little kit. There was a little road map of the surrounding streets so I could find my way out, some cash, and he'd also put in the handle of an old shaver so that I could get my handcuffs off, that old type of shaver that had a metal screw that fit perfectly in the old-style Halcón handcuffs. He brought me the shoes and said, "Look, if they take you to hospital, you'll be taken somewhere near here, I already checked it out, and from there you have to come out over here, you'll come across this wall here, and you'll be able to jump it because I tried and I can jump it fine, so you'll have no problems." Which is to say that my father had already tested out the route inside the hospital, he'd marked exactly where I needed to go, where I'd have to scale a fence, and he even scaled it himself, to see if it was possible. And at this point he was already seventy-something years old.

And how did the escape go?

The escape failed. I swallowed the razor blades and I was taken to hospital. They took an X-ray and confirmed that in effect, the razor blades were in my stomach, but they didn't leave me there. They sent me back to the prison to have my operation at a later date. In the meantime, in the part of the prison next to my cell—each cell held five prisoners—some of the guys had busted through the floor and found that the earth underneath was soft, so they could dig a tunnel. At first it was pretty messy, but later, when others saw that the digging was progressing, they came to help. But eventually someone turned them in. The screws came and found the tunnel. You can imagine what an escape attempt from a loony bin looks like; there must be a thousand jokes about it. So, when they asked my four cellmates to make a statement about the tunnel, they all said things like "I was just building an en suite" or "The thing is, I was being called by aliens from the other side." That was the end of the tunnel, but there was a general search of the cells, and they found my shoes. So they all got away with the tunnel business but I got busted for my shoes. I was put in the hole for two weeks: that was the end of my escape plan.

<u>What's it like to swallow twenty-seven razor blades?</u>
<u>How does it feel?</u>

You don't feel anything. When you do something like that, you don't do it thinking that you're going to die or you're going to tear yourself up inside. You do it because you want something. It's a means to an end.

<u>Did it hurt?</u>

No. In fact, they never had to operate on me. I got them out without any problems.

<u>You shat them out?</u>

Yeah, it's not so tricky. Besides, there was the haloperidol.

There are worse things. I had a cellmate who ate a whole sheet of glass. From a window. I'm talking about those old windows, with the wires inside them. Well, he ate the whole thing. Chewed it and all.

Why, though?

As a form of protest, or because he'd lost it. I remember there was a guy who had killed his parents—it was a famous case, he had made quite a name for himself. He died in Unit 20; he didn't last very long. He came in suffering from something from the outside; he'd been on the streets. Long story short, he plucked his own eyes out. Pulled them right out, with his fingers. Then he died. He let himself die; you could tell he didn't want to live anymore.

Self-harm is very common. We have a guy here now, he spends his whole life cutting himself, every day. They're just superficial cuts; he doesn't go too crazy on himself. His arms are all cut up and now he's starting on his chest. The other day he cut a couple of crosses into his chest. I told him he was halfway toward a game of tic-tac-toe. If he kept on with Xs and Os every time he cut himself, soon he'd have a game of tic-tac-toe.

19

When did the Devil come into your religious practice?

Santería is difficult to explain. It involves earth spirits and light spirits. The earth spirits are what in Christianity you'd call devils. Many of them lived on Earth at one time, and so their evil is of this world, the deceit of this world. There are *candomblés* [songs] from the Quimbanda religion that name Pomba Gira as Lucifer's wife. Pomba Gira has seven personalities, as does Tranca Rua. Pomba Gira is a spirit commonly used for protection by those involved in prostitution, and by transvestites, the same way that criminals have Saint Death or Tranca Rua, the spirit who opens pathways. Tranca Rua is the lord of all roads, he is always in cemeteries, he handles souls. Just like Saint Death, they are pagan saints who act as intermediaries between the living and the spirits.

Well, for me, I never sought intermediaries; I don't have

a spirit who connects me to something higher. I would go straight to the source. With my beliefs I didn't want to fall into the sort of mysticism my mother practiced at the time.

I don't see the Devil as an evil being. I would say that the word "devil" has been demonized. I see the Devil more as a powerful being who helps those who believe in him.

Christianity is a religion driven by fear. I accept Lucifer because he preferred to be a king in hell rather than a slave in heaven. Perhaps though, in my day-to-day, my normal behavior, my way of thinking . . . Perhaps I'm more of a Christian than anything else. But that doesn't mean that Lucifer rejects me. Your own faith is one thing, and what others expect from you is quite another. For me religion is one thing, and my behavior is another. I don't mix them.

In fact, in all these years, I've had lots of dealings with Christians. I had a Christian sponsor, a sponsor from Cáritas who came especially to see me. The people from Cáritas who came to Unit 20 brought *alfajores*, cigarettes, yerba maté, cakes, soda, soap. They knew that everyone in Unit 20 was considered a pariah, and that a lot of us went hungry, and so they tried to improve that. When we were moved here they stopped coming, because the guards steal everything: the food, the nice soda.

Thanks to this sponsor from Cáritas, I have a very special trophy. In my religious ceremonies I use a cup for certain things, for certain offerings. For the ceremony, it's important that the cup be made of metal. And for the very last Mass they held in Unit 20, before they closed it, Cáritas brought along Cardinal Bergoglio [now Pope Francis]. Several TV channels came too—my sponsor introduced me to Bergoglio, we spoke for a while, and then he gave me the chalice he had used to celebrate Mass.

He gave it to you for your ceremonies? I mean, did he know what you were going to use it for?

Yeah, he gave it to me so I could use it in my ceremonies. My sponsor had told him what I got up to, I don't know—but Bergoglio gave it to me all the same.

So what you're saying is, you have the Pope's chalice and you use it to worship Lucifer and other spirits?

Yeah. It's a cup in the form of a chalice, very simple, unornamented.

Can you describe the look on Bergoglio's face while you were chatting and he started to realize that you prayed to the Devil?

Oh, it wasn't like that at all, he was very chill. He's from the Franciscan order, he's not a regular priest. It's a different way of thinking. I respect him because he's very respectful in the way he treats others. And there was that time he washed the feet of all the nutjobs. He picked out the worst nutjobs we had, people who were completely destroyed. It's not like they rounded up the best ones for a little ceremony. The guy went and found the worst of them.

(. . .)

When I pray, more than anything I give thanks. It's like

going to a psychologist: you get a problem out in the open to work on it better. Although I live here in this shit, I have an anchor that helps me with the day-to-day, that gives me strength, peace, and serenity to go on, and I'm thankful for that.

I'm not one for invocations, because I don't think that prison is the place for that. It's a very dark place. All of the energy in this place is evil; it's a place of madness, pain, and suffering. If you summon something here, you'll only bring suffering, you'll call upon the darkest things in these surroundings. So I make no invocations. I give thanks and I pray, but I don't make invocations. I've had many cellmates who fool around in here: "Hey, let's play the game with the cup," and things like that. No. Not even as a joke, not in here.

Outside, in a temple, I'd celebrate the proper days, I'd make the proper offerings of drinks, with the correct mix. In here, because I don't have the right ingredients or the opportunity to go to the right place to do it, I offer what I have and what I can. And perhaps my offerings are more impassioned and truer than those I could make on the outside. If I spend a week without smoking so that I can offer cigarettes, or I give up eating something that is very important to me, like a chocolate that's very difficult to get ahold of, it's an offering of my sacrifice. I'm giving something that is very difficult to obtain, because in here whatever I offer has great value. I offer up something that hurts to be without.

What's more, it's something I see the whole time I'm fasting, because it sits there on the altar all day, right in front of me.

What happens to the offerings? Do they stay there on the altar?

The altar gets cleaned once a month. When I was in Unit 20, I could burn the offerings. Here, unfortunately, there's nowhere to burn anything, so I throw them away. I use lots of packaged things, because the altar is in my cell, next to my bed, and it'd be crawling with bugs. In the outside world, offerings are left in town squares, on the ground, beneath trees.

Speaking of your altar . . . What about using documents to protect against the souls of your victims? Do you still do that?

No, I don't do that anymore. I can't remember the photos of the people I killed. I don't recall ever having seen their faces. Their spirits never came to bother me or demand anything from me.

At this stage, there's only one thing I'm going to try to take care of. Not in terms of my thoughts, but—well, the thing is, to try . . . not to hurt anyone with my memories.

What do you mean by that?

[Melogno reflects for a few seconds.]

The victims had families. You understand what I'm saying, right? I don't want to offend those people.

Did you ever hear anything from any of the families?

No. But just in case, I want to be very clear. Beyond all the excuses, all the—not excuses, the mitigating factors that there might be in my case—I did commit those murders.

Are you making a sort of moral evaluation about it all?

There's no evaluation, these are facts.

In terms of reincarnation, have you ever thought you might come across those taxi drivers? Have you ever fantasized about that?

We will all meet again at some point. So the answer is yes. It's not something I fantasize about, it's something that will definitely happen. But I also believe that there will be no judgment on the other side, because those men are already living other lives. And that goes for me too—after I die, I'll be someone else. In every reincarnation you come across the same people; that's why when you have a strange affinity with someone, often it's because . . . The thing is, the person who is your lover today, in the next reincarnation, they could be your brother. Or your butcher.

20

In the federal capital of Buenos Aires, I can't be charged, because I was deemed incapable of comprehending my actions. But in Buenos Aires Province I was deemed fit for trial, and as a consequence, I am responsible for my actions. The Justice Department of Buenos Aires Province should be given the Nobel Prize in psychiatry, because they found the cure for schizophrenia: all you have to do is cross General Paz Avenue.

The key issue, and my main problem in judicial terms, is the lack of motive for my crimes. If I had said that I killed in order to steal money, I would have been set free fifteen years ago. Or even if I said I did it for pleasure. At least there'd be a logic to it. But I don't recall any reason or anything that set me off. There was no precedent.

I have nothing against taxi drivers. I never felt hatred

for taxi drivers. They never wronged me, nobody in my family had anything against taxi drivers, and I wasn't worried about the color or make of the taxis either. I couldn't tell you exactly why I chose the people I did.

For my case, the forensic medical teams invented the term "potential dangerousness." It has since been applied to other cases too. It's possible it was used previously, but the first time it appears in writing was for my case. What is "potential dangerousness"? Well, it's the idea that although I'm perfectly fine and calm today, no one knows what might happen tomorrow.

When I was deemed unfit for trial, they made me sign a statement: "Free of guilt and charge, with good name and honor unsullied, at the pleasure of the Federal Penitentiary Service until his dangerousness disappears." Now, in legal terms, "dangerousness" could last anywhere between a day and a hundred years, depending on the forensic medical team. If the forensic medical team don't like the sound of your answers, you stay right where you are.

(...)

Over the years, they've diagnosed me as everything except oligophrenic. Borderline, psychopath, psychotic, schizophrenic, autistic, paraphrenic. I've gone through every psychiatric state there is. I ended up with the worst one, where they diagnosed me with a psychopathic personality, which means that at the root of my personality there is psychopathy that can never be cured. I can live perfectly well without medication, but this doesn't mean I'm not considered a dangerous person, and in the report presented to the judicial panels I'm described as a predator waiting for the moment to attack. My response to that is this: I must be the dumbest predator in the world; otherwise, why would I have let thirty years go by in jail without killing anyone? Fine, I might be waiting for a particular victim, but thirty years without lifting a finger? Am I that particular? And here I am in the best place in the world for someone who wants to be violent.

(. . .)

Unfortunately, for a very long time I was very wrong-headed. Besides the acts that I committed themselves, at a certain point I realized that the grim fascination surrounding the murders created a space for me. I used my dangerousness as a calling card. I liked the look of disgust on people's faces when I talked about certain things, and so I got to exaggerating or changing details in my stories.

There was one judge, a professor at the university, who visited for many years, bringing his new students, twenty or thirty of them each time, to speak to me. When I told my story and the guy thought I was toning it down a bit, he'd spur me on a little: "Ricardo, tell my students how you committed your murders, how you *watched* the bodies *crumple*. Tell them about the blood, Ricardo." I watched the expressions on those people's faces and then I'd exaggerate. The judge looked after me well; he was very friendly.

After our meetings, he'd take the students on a little tour of Unit 20, so they'd get to see what a madhouse looks like. One day, when the visit with the students was over, one of the psychiatrists from my team came to get me and take me back to my cell, but she pretended like she was being careless and let me trail behind the professor as he left, so I could eavesdrop. He had no idea I was listening there behind him, and he spoke to the group as they left the building: "The day you meet a monster, you'll know it straightaway, because what you just saw in there was a monster." My mistake was not protecting myself from harmful attention. It pisses me off that those people left feeling happy, feeling superior, because they had a monster with which to compare themselves. It hurts that I was the one to gift them that moment.

I think that was related to another issue, the question of being heard and accepted. People paid attention to me during those visits. And I participated in the discussion like an actor reading a script. I bought into the charade because people paid attention to me, and then to hold their attention I added a few details to the facts.

What sort of details?

Like taking blood from the victims, things like that. I'd change things up, I'd take in the look of fear on their faces and sort of improvise.

(. . .)

After thirty years of psychiatric treatment, I still don't

understand how they can come up with a diagnosis with sketches and inkblots. Because at the end of the day it's still all up to the subjective opinion of whoever is administering the tests. "Melogno, what do you see here?" "A lighter." "But you must see something else." "Why?" "Melogno, what do you see here?" "An inkblot." It's just an inkblot, why do I *have to see something* in an inkblot?

So occasionally, just to get along, you say something. And then, most of the time, they use what you've said to sink you.

For a while I had this fantasy that I'd like to go and live down south. In one of these interviews, the doctor asked me why. "Because there are no people there," I said. "I'd be calm there. And if I had some kind of episode, I'd just kill a cow, not a person." The son of a bitch wrote down that I wanted to move to the south to kill cows.

The last time I underwent testing in Buenos Aires Province . . . after all these years, some of my psychiatrists here know the ones over there, and my psychiatrist here told me that their psychologist noticed with surprise that when they gave me their sheets of paper to take the tests, I took them and shuffled them in a way she had never seen before in any textbook. I don't how people take pieces of paper and shuffle them in textbooks.

In general, it's rare that they give you the results of their studies. They tell you "it didn't go well" but they don't tell you why.

They understand that if you see the results, you'll learn how to better handle things next time.

(. . .)

Many years ago, a psychiatrist told me that it was incredible that, considering what I'd done, there were no physical signs in my brain of what happened. I don't fully understand it, but it seems there ought to have been some kind of trace or mark left behind. But I don't have one. A psychotic break of the type I am supposed to have suffered leaves a mark on the brain, and that ought to be visible.

In the nineties they took a tomogram of me in the Ramos Mejía Hospital. Next to the machine there was a sign that said No Metal Objects and they took my tomogram while I was handcuffed with a warden next to me with a gun and a bulletproof vest on. The results came out fine, as if my brain were healthy.

Three or four years ago they took another tomogram, in slightly better circumstances, and again, my brain was fine.

Currently, I have no issues of comprehension from a legal standpoint. I am fit for trial. I've suffered no psychotic breaks in thirty-four years of incarceration. I haven't taken psychiatric medication in years. I've been examined physically and apart from the diabetes and degenerative osteoarthritis, I'm in perfect health.

But the forensic medical team says that given that my basic structure hasn't changed, and that I have no social container (a social container means a family on the outside), this makes me potentially dangerous. They sort of see it from the perspective that if you have a family, the family will look after you.

They mention my chronic solitary behavior: that if I'm alone I'll think a lot, and if I think a lot I will become disturbed, and if I become disturbed . . . I'll commit crimes.

Statistically Unusual

[*M.R. is a psychiatrist. She treated Ricardo for seven years in Unit 20 of the Borda Hospital.*]

Strange in what sense?

<u>He doesn't seem like a serial killer.</u>

Were you expecting someone in a leather mask, carrying a chainsaw?

<u>Maybe not that exactly, but . . . he seems more like a pencil pusher than a serial killer.</u>

Haha, it's not a bad image, the poor guy.

<u>Is he, in fact, a serial killer?</u>

Considering there were four murders, that the victims and methodology follow a specific pattern, and that there is a certain spacing between incidents, you could say the answer is yes. But going by what Ricardo has said, one important element that defines a serial killer is missing, and that's the period where the homicidal impulse between crimes recedes. He speaks of an inertia, a slightly more continuous impulse.

Apart from that, with serial killings, generally there

are elements that evolve from murder to murder. "Series" means a succession of terms that vary from a fixed base. There's a fixed element, but this element evolves in some aspects. In this case, rather than a series, it's more like the same crime repeated four times, almost identically.

For me, this almost falls outside the existing classifications for multiple homicides. Of course, these definitions are poor as well, because the studies are made from a very small sample set. Very strange people, very unusual in statistical terms. In a normal distribution of the total population, murderers we might deem "irrational," those who don't kill for pedestrian reasons like jealousy or money are right at the end of the curve. It's a tiny population in numerical terms. And Ricardo . . . well, I'd say if you put together a Gaussian distribution that only featured irrational murderers, Ricardo would be on the extreme of that curve too. He's a very unusual person, even when considered within a population of unusual people.

<u>What makes him so unusual?</u>

First, there's the series of contradictory diagnoses across the years. They've been contradictory and they've never quite described him fully. Second, there's the lack of motive for his actions, and the impossibility of inferring them. His lack of deterioration is also noteworthy. Nearly every diagnosis he's been given implies functional deterioration over time, which he doesn't show. Every diagnosis except psychopathy.

<u>Is he a psychopath?</u>

Personally, having treated him for several years, I don't think so. In terms of concrete behavior, he's not a predator, he's not a parasite. He has a certain degree of empathy—I've seen him become upset hearing about the circumstances of others; I've seen him help out. If a psychopath talks to you, it's to use you, or because they want to enjoy something they're about to do to you. That's not the case with Ricardo. He's not manipulative, he's not a liar. He tells you exactly what's going on, and often he'll tell you things that aren't in his best interest. My interpretation of this is that he's on the autism spectrum. He responds in concrete terms. You ask him something and he answers. He understands things literally, and he responds literally to whatever you ask him. In fact, he makes an effort to find an answer.

<u>So why is there this diagnosis of psychopathy?</u>

When they found no delirious responses, when they failed to see him in a psychotic state—he doesn't rant or rave, or speak incoherently—some medical professionals took this to mean he was a psychopath. He's intelligent, if that's something that can be associated with psychopaths. And that's where the fact that he's respectful and on good terms with prison staff comes in: sometimes psychiatrists see this as a sign of psychopathic adaptation, but that's a very weak argument.

The last time he was diagnosed with psychopathy in the courts in the Province of Buenos Aires was relatively recently, just when the courts in the City of Buenos Aires lifted their safety restrictions on him and he could begin to ask for supervised excursions. Then the Province declared he had a contracted illness. For them Ricardo had been normal all this time, conscious and responsible for his actions.

An illness contracted from what?

From his time in prison. An illness he theoretically contracted in prison, and which prevents him from leaving. In other words, according to them, he recently acquired, as an adult, an illness, psychopathy, which in fact is not an illness—it's a stable condition that doesn't change. They diagnosed him with it out of fear, because they were going to have to let him out, and they were too afraid to sign off on his release.

With regards to his inability to show emotions: I don't know what they want, to see him going around trying to kiss everyone perhaps. He's an older man, he's spent his whole life in prison, in shitty places, surviving among crazy people, constantly being examined.

There is one very noteworthy factor, no small matter, which is his lack of injuries in prison. It's very strange, and I must stress *very* strange, for an individual to have suffered no wounds from fighting with other inmates in over thirty-five years of jail time.

Have you observed him interact with other prisoners?

Yes. When I met him he was already older; he had

established himself inside and everyone treated him with respect. Some of the jailbirds even called him "Don Ricardo" and spoke to him very respectfully. The young ones who were the most volatile treated him with sensible friendliness. People asked for his advice, and he even adjudicated minor disputes.

What about the other diagnoses? In the notes from 1982 they make mention of the possibility of schizophrenia.

No—he's not schizophrenic. It's one of the few possibilities that I can dismiss out of hand, because never before have we seen a schizophrenic who is able to cure themselves, or who over time doesn't suffer a notable decline in function, which is not the case for Ricardo. If Ricardo were schizophrenic, by now his condition would have greatly deteriorated. They even diagnosed him with Borderline Personality Disorder, but I see no signs of it in him: he doesn't fall apart emotionally, he's never cut himself, he doesn't have that borderline vulnerability in the face of emotions or circumstances. He works, and he has continuity in his work life.

There's the paraphrenia diagnosis, as well. I am pretty much in agreement with that diagnosis.

What is paraphrenia?

It's not quite schizophrenia, but it still has nasty manifestations. A schizophrenic patient tends to stick to one side: if they have a persecution fantasy, they are more likely to involve others in this fantasy, including their therapist.

A paraphrenic patient tends to live between the two poles of fantasy and reality.

I've treated many paraphrenics, mostly women. One of them told me she received messages from an alien mothership. When I asked her why I couldn't hear these messages, her response was, "But Doctor! It's because you don't have the antenna!" as she pointed at my head. She believed she did have the antenna. In all other respects she was a normal, functioning person: she was a mother, a housewife, and while she complained a little bit about her husband, who was a bit obsessive about tidiness, there was nothing more serious than that. But if you brought up the alien mothership, she'd go off the deep end. She was a very friendly woman, and she managed to live without conflict between these two worlds.

Ricardo isn't psychotic either, because in general a psychotic patient needs some form of medication to prevent breaks or episodes, and it has been many years since he took psychiatric medication. Whatever he has or had, it's not something that produces a deficit or requires medication for him to be balanced and well.

But it remains unclear how Ricardo's mechanism for stabilization works, or how he managed to be in the condition he is in now. It must have something to do with the combination of treatment plans, the deliberate overmedicating, being locked up, having order imposed from outside. This evolution took place over the course of decades in real shitholes, in truly atrocious circumstances. Unit 20 was the sort of lunatic asylum you see in horror movies; it was somewhere people were dumped and forgotten. It wasn't the sort of place to stimulate any kind of recovery.

Just a moment ago you said that Ricardo might be on the autism spectrum?

That's because of everything he has told me about his social difficulties, his problems at school, all that stuff about talking to himself and gesticulating, losing himself in his own world. His way of living between the real world and his own fantasy world. It's very likely that for much of his childhood and adolescence he was on the autism spectrum. He had good coping mechanisms, but he was on the spectrum. For people like him, engaging with the outside always brings tension, and causes them to be on the alert. This tension could explain, at least in part, his early flight toward a world of fantasy, because in that fantasy world he is in control and can anticipate what will happen. This is much more comfortable than reality, which is unpredictable and generally more threatening.

He never fantasized about killing, but there was a connection between his fantasy world and the crimes. He said that losing himself in that other world meant that he lost control in this one. What is he referring to here? Control over what? There doesn't seem to be a strong link to the murders. How does he go from the fantasy world to killing?

From what Ricardo has said, he became increasingly

disconnected from reality, and he tried to slip away from it more and more each day. This slipping away was a form of control; it took control of him. The fantasies increase as contact with reality is lost. He fantasized about himself, which was something he had done since childhood. Gradually he became lost in this fantasy world that was something like a comic book: he was a shogun, he went on adventures. I think he must have had some kind of psychotic episode in childhood, which is where the notion of feeling presences might come from. He talks about how as a child, he slept with a knife under his pillow, that he was afraid of the dark, of what was under the bed. Childhood fears like these are normal; all kids experience them. But not many kids sleep with a knife under their pillow. I think he crosses a line there.

In this case, Ricardo's fantasies don't mean the same thing as what we usually see in a classic case of serial killing, where a murderer fantasizes for long periods of time beforehand about killing or torture, and has already sown the seed of ritual through the pleasure taken in thinking about or planning the crime. The plan itself is a sort of erotic pleasure. For Ricardo there was no plan, no pleasure.

So, what about the link between the murders and his fantasy world? The most reasonable explanation is to suppose that Ricardo had a brief psychotic episode. If that was the case, for the duration of the episode his two worlds melded and fused together. I believe that while that happened, Ricardo was not present in reality, that is to say the reality that we all more or less share.

Wasn't the execution of his killings too organized to have taken place while experiencing a psychotic break?

Haha, yes—that's if you consider living in the street, going to the cinema every afternoon to watch the same film six times, then wandering around like a robot all day with a loaded pistol in your bag "organized."

But generally, aren't crimes committed during psychotic breaks extremely violent? Here the method seems to be quite restrained.

Yes, that's the classic scenario with a psychotic break: very violent crimes where someone mutilates bodies, gouges out eyes, and writes on the walls in blood. But that's not always the case.

In Ricardo's version of events, there doesn't seem to be any evolution in his illness, something that grows worse and leads to the murders.

No. But we're talking about many elements that we can't know about for sure. He doesn't remember the crimes, and there's no one left who can speak to how things were for him back then. Although he doesn't mention it, I believe that his fantasy world must have grown stronger and stronger. It must have expanded up until a breaking point, and then even that breaking point is lost on Ricardo. The lack of memory itself is a clue, an indication of a psychotic break.

<u>Does reaching a breaking point imply a buildup of tension or energy in some part of him?</u>

When Ricardo says that he dealt well with military service, I'm not totally surprised. Military service simplifies things a great deal. Once you learn the rules, you have a bed and something to eat, and there's not much to think about besides following those rules. It's a system in which everything is laid out very clearly. And what's more, he could arrange his life so that he could get by while maintaining his fantasy world. However, until he could get his head around the rules, it must have been very stressful. He doesn't say anything about that period, but I feel it must have been very tense until he understood the rules and adapted to them.

Then, afterward, he got out of the army and went back to the real world, which is much more demanding. The real world had changed; the times were tough [due to the economic crisis following the Malvinas conflict]. These are the circumstances that led Ricardo's father to put together the business for him, to say "you're in charge" and to give a pistol to a young man in no condition, at that stage, to manage anything. I believe all of this must have created a highly stressful environment for Ricardo.

When the demands of a certain environment become too much, anyone can have a psychotic break. And because of his background as a person with low tolerance to change or uncertainty, Ricardo was already more susceptible to such a break. The fact that he wore his uniform when he didn't need to could be interpreted as a way of dressing himself up in a previous sense of order, of trying to hold on to an identity that was slipping away.

Another strange point is the motive for the murders.

Yes. Every killer has a motive, even if the motive is crazy. Sometimes there are false motives, or a motive a killer is lying about, for example. But here there's nothing.

Generally, in crimes like these, there's a deranged, almost novelistic rationale at play. But even within the hallucination or the paranoia, there's some sort of logic. And then usually the logic of the delirium gives you the tools to reconstruct the real mechanism that triggered the incident. There's none of that in Ricardo's case either—there's just a void where that should be.

A delirium can help you to interpret who the killer truly wanted to murder, or what they were seeking to destroy. Because in these cases the deranged person is always moving toward something concrete: it's not like they attack just any random individual. Usually this takes the form of trying to destroy something from within, themselves in another person. And in this case, so clearly repeated, he tried to destroy the same thing four times. We might ask ourselves what he wanted to kill, what it was he wanted to completely destroy. Something that those others had. What was it that those taxi drivers represented, that Ricardo wanted to kill?

This is a strange case when it comes to unsolved crimes.

The murderer is in jail, and the where, when, how, and who are clearly established. But we have no idea why.

That's right. There is a jumble of probable causes, none of which completely satisfy the question of why. We still don't know what *really happened* there. What was the exchange? There is, inevitably, a mechanism somewhere that explains everything. But with so many holes in the available information, and without any further facts or information that may surface, it seems unlikely at this stage that we'll ever know for sure.

How does the figure of the mother influence all of this?

In general, she wasn't a benign influence, that's for sure. She was someone who twisted things around in Ricardo's head, beyond any question of illnesses or special conditions that he might have been suffering. She didn't help him at all, and she contributed to his sense of fear during childhood. Beyond that, the acts of murder don't seem to be directed toward her, at least not directly.

Then there were his four suicide attempts during childhood. And four murders. The comments about all men being botched abortions. I'm not saying you can rule it out, but it's much more complicated than simply killing the mother.

And related to that, there's a connection between childhood and the murders: the disposal of the bodies. The places where he killed.

He says he didn't know the addresses he gave to the taxi drivers, that they were places chosen as if by chance.

Yes, but when I first met him—I knew nothing about him, and I had no memory of his case in the papers—I was curious and I went to the National Library to read the newspapers from 1982 to see if I could dig anything up, and there was a little map of the streets in the neighborhood and the places where the bodies were found.

That's right. It's from when they were still searching for the killer. They mapped out the three dead bodies in Mataderos and the two attempted assaults that weren't committed by Ricardo.

Exactly. So, the three dead bodies are grouped around the house where Ricardo grew up with his mother; they're very close. The farthest one was only four blocks away.

So those were actually the last three murders. What about the first one? Did you discuss that with him?

Not directly. I asked him a few questions but he didn't seem to register them. So, about the first murder? I don't know. It's a bit farther away, but not that far. Seems like it happened a bit closer to the house where he lived with his father. This could line up with the habit in autistic people of only moving about in routine, familiar places. Or it could indicate something else entirely.

Is there any link between the crimes and his approach to religion and spirits, et cetera?

Those are parallel issues, I think. One the one hand, he keeps the identity documents of the drivers so that their spirits won't haunt him, but on the other, I don't think that he killed for religious reasons. He takes religious precautions, but that comes after the crimes.

His sense of religion is all he has left from his mother, the only element of protection that he could identify and take from her. The entities he uses in his current religious practices are all protective entities. They have nothing to do with Saint Death or Gauchito Gil, which you learn in prison. They are things he learned from his maternal line. In this sense religion looms very large, it's a strong part of his makeup, but it doesn't strike me as a direct cause for the crimes—it's more a parallel thing.

He's very serious in his religious practice. At least he was at the time when I knew him. He had a pentacle drawn on the floor of his cell, with strange drawings all around it, and every Friday he would spend the whole night sitting in the middle of it, praying.

That's also how things are in prison: mysticism is very common. If you don't hold on to something, you end up killing yourself, or going crazy. Or going even more crazy.

What about Ricardo killing cats?

That's what people said about him. But they also said he could levitate. I don't know, I only ever saw him with one cat, and he had him for many years. His name was Rigoberto. He was the cat who said hello.

What do you mean he said hello?

Oh, it was just a silly thing. Ricardo would say "Say hello, Rigoberto," and the cat would look at him first, then he'd look at you and say "meow." Ricardo used to say he wasn't just a cat. He used to sit nearly the whole day in the middle of the pentacle.

Could we say that for Ricardo, the murders represented a twisted kind of therapy? This rupture, this jumble of events, didn't it free him in a certain sense? Didn't it bring him calm?

That's something that many Lacanians say: the movement from thought to action is an attempt to break through a subjective dead end. It's the desire to break through an unbearable environment to reach a new level of stability. Individuals cast themselves out of a place. They jump, and land where they land.

But in Ricardo's version of events, we never see this "unbearable environment."

No, we don't. But something must have become unbearable. He talks about needing to go "nowhere." Four murders don't just happen by themselves. Always, and even more clearly in cases like these, a killing or an act of violence is the search for balance, for the release of tension.

At such a point, this idea that he would arrive at a new level of equilibrium . . . Note that right in the middle of the week he committed the murders he came across that woman, the lady who kind of mistreated him, and all of a sudden, he sees her as smaller. The first time you hear that anecdote, you might think that Ricardo was hallucinating, that he felt that he had become larger. I like to think of it the other way: that he wasn't hallucinating after the murders, but before them. Before, he saw that woman as larger, stronger than she was, but after the murders, he saw her as she truly was.

<u>What is the likelihood that he would have continued killing if he hadn't been arrested?</u>

That's a controversial question. There are people who say he'd already stopped, that it had been over two weeks since his last murder when they locked him up. I have my reservations about that. If someone has a psychotic break, it's difficult for them to come back without medication, without confinement. There's a common saying in psychiatry: walls—of the hospital, or the prison—hold things in. They hold in everything a patient's head can't. A psychiatrist and a psychologist are also a kind of container, a dike for the mental structures that are falling down, that become blurred and confuse reality with fantasy.

<u>Is he still dangerous?</u>

Well, let's see. He's stable. He's not a violent person and he hasn't shown any predatory behavior in over thirty years. I don't think he'd do what he did again, given the same circumstances. Of course, he is still capable of killing, but by now the probability that he would kill would be about the same as for you or me. Have you ever seriously fantasized about killing someone?

<u>Of course.</u>

Good. Me too. And I'll tell you something else: when

I say I fantasize about killing, I'm talking about killing a specific, actual person. A person with a first and last name. Someone I know very well. Twice a month I go to a shooting range. I'm no crack shot, but I make do. I can group my shots together tightly. Every time I go, I use up two boxes of bullets. And each time I pull the trigger, I'm thinking of that person. Now, I'm not actually planning to physically kill them when I do this. But each time I shoot at a target, in my mind I'm shooting that person right in the head. Four boxes of .22 caliber bullets every month. If we look at the facts, Ricardo committed four murders, and I've committed none. But in the current situation, it's possible I'm more dangerous than he is. And yet here we are, chatting away.

Electricity and Magnetism

September 1982. The dead of night, at a dark crossroads in Lomas del Mirador. On one of the four corners, there's a taxi parked a few centimeters away from the sidewalk. Inside the car, for a brief moment, the passage of time has somehow come to a halt.

The taxi driver is dead. There's a bullet in his head and his body is slumped in the front seat, leaning toward the passenger side. At the edge of the scene, in the back seat, a young man around twenty years old holds a .22 caliber pistol that's still smoking. He's paralyzed with terror: he has just discovered that he is being *observed*. From the rearview mirror, strange eyes stare at him intensely.

While this instant remains frozen in time, a correspondence is produced between these two gazes. On the watery film covering the eyes watching him from the mirror, he is reflected dark and convex in the interior of the taxi. In miniature, above the center of the pupils, you can see the face of the young passenger who stares on, hypnotized, at the rearview mirror, like a deer caught in headlights that shatter the darkness of the night. If you could zoom in to his pupils, once more you would see the reflection of those eyes watching him from the rearview mirror. Inside the eyes, the young man's face again, and so on: one image inside another image, a series of reflections opposing one another. Reality itself shrinking away.

21

We all have this wish to turn back time and do things differently, but we're also the sum of what we do in our lives. Unfortunately, that's the way it is. If I had the opportunity to change everything that led me to be in jail, I would. But I also know that for better or worse, jail was my salvation. Being thrown all of a sudden inside four walls, where there's a different way of living, hardened me up a lot; it forced me to find the strength to live. Before that, I was weak.

We've established that haloperidol is bullshit, and that the treatment you receive at the hands of the prison system is bullshit too, but in my case, something good came from— they brought me out of—you could say, They brought me back to reality. I grew up here, I became strong, I learned to defend myself. The medication and the treatment helped, even if it meant I spent years fucked up or in a daze.

(. . .)

Something that kept me, uh, sane . . . was the lack of visitors. After my father stopped coming, no one else ever visited. That forced me to survive, to get by on my own. I see that as something that helped me. Nobody relied on me. Nobody was waiting for me on the outside. That always helped.

(. . .)

At the moment I'm a bit of a problem, because no one thought I'd survive as long as I have, that I'd last this long and in this condition. In here I'm a dinosaur.

I've never stolen from another inmate. I never took anyone out. I never pushed anyone's buttons. That's why wherever I go I have friends, people who remember me. If some kid says to someone, "That old guy slapped me," they'll tell him, "You must have deserved it, because I know that guy, I know what he's like." In the thirty-four years I've spent in prison, the only visible injury I suffered was this one [*Melogno shows his forearms, where there are twenty or so small, circular scars*]. Rubber bullets from an Ithaca shotgun, from a scuffle in Unit 20. One of the guards was trying to shoot me in the head, but he was really short, so when I put my arms up, he got me here.

(. . .)

Within the prison system, there are many people I appreciate. People who, despite this shit-show all around us, still treated me well. Bosses, like the guy who gave me my first job. Teachers, people who bothered to show me how to do certain jobs I had no skills for. Some of the professionals too, the psychiatrists and the psychologists. Some of the guards, who had and still have good relations with me. But despite all this, I still have a jailer–prisoner relationship with all these teachers and people who I appreciate and who appreciate me. No matter how well you get along, no matter how much they respect you, when the shit hits the fan they're going to side with their own people. That's their duty, their job; it's their people. So I wouldn't say I have any friends among the prison staff. If a guy has to stick it to you, he's going to stick it to you.

Over my years in jail I gained a level of respect and a situation that, like it or not, has allowed me to live a little better inside. In Unit 20, I began by working in the laundry, and in the kitchen sometimes. In the laundry they had a huge industrial washer. In the summer I'd fill the drum with water and use it like a jacuzzi. In the dead of night I'd get in, and I'd drink a cold juice from the kitchen. I made those moments and opportunities happen. I even had an electronics workshop for a number of years, where I'd fix anything in the unit that was broken.

Here you have your sense of calm, a bigger room, better food, but it's worse off for you in a judicial sense. There are fewer visits, there's less money floating around, and there aren't as many drugs as in the other cellblocks.

It's like anywhere: you have your advantages and disadvantages.

I have my tape recorder, my TV, my little fan. I have everything I need right here in my cell. I have running water, I have a toilet. I have everything except a shower. I could live locked up in here. Right here in this cell, I mean.

At the moment I'm waiting for a new DVD player because cockroaches broke the last one I had. Cockroaches ruin everything. It's completely infested in here, like the rest of the jail. A cockroach seeks heat. They don't eat your TV, but they build their little nests in there between the elements and once you short-circuit, you're screwed. Tiny little cockroaches, making their nests in your DVD player. I come in here at night and I have to ask their permission to lie down in my own bed. They crawl over the walls, they're everywhere.

(. . .)

I'm fifty-four years old. The kids see me and give me shit: "Hey old man, you must have been real bad in your day, but now . . ." They think I'm old and fat. But then I show them I can do this. [*Melogno stands and after a series of awkward movements, he is standing up and touching his forehead with the heel of his foot.*] The kids see that and say, "Look at that old son of a bitch!" and I just say, "I'm not fat yet—I'll be fat the day I can no longer do this." I also get on the floor and sit in the lotus position, I get on my knees and stretch, I splay my fingers out and do push-ups using just my fingers. Then I make a fist and do push-ups, punching the ground each time I go down. I do all this in my cell with the door open. That way they see that despite my age, and my weight, they still have to respect me. It's a survival thing too. They see you haven't gone completely to waste and that if they take you on, there'll be something coming their way.

Have you ever come across someone who didn't know who you are?

Yes. But they soon find out [*laughter*]. On top of your actual sentence, rumors fly around too. Also, let's say you have a disagreement with one guy—later on the others will go and tell him what's what. You're up there with your reputation. Whoever comes to fuck with you, as long as they aren't fully loaded.

What does "fully loaded" mean?

That's when other people fill someone's head with ideas so that they come and blow up in your face. So, as long as a guy hasn't been put up to it, and doesn't have a serious issue or a personal problem with you, he's going to be afraid of you even when he tries to take you on.

I'm more of a teacher, in that sense. Just like I was taught back in my time, I'm someone who likes to teach and explain how things are. If I see that there's a conflict brewing, I confront the person alone. Because if you do it in front of everyone, it's a bigger deal and you have to win because everyone's watching, so if you back out they'll fuck you up. But when it's one on one, there's a different level of negotiation.

I'm the type to punch a guy in the chest, because that's the sort of hit where you can feel . . . power. Or high on the head. That's a hit that doesn't do too much damage and it leaves no traces. If you give a guy a black eye, he's going to have to cop it from everyone: "Hey, nice shiner," et cetera, and then he's going to be obliged to get vengeance so he doesn't lose face. I've seen guys burnt with oil. A guy who lost a fight went off and boiled the oil, waited for the other guy to go to sleep, and then poured it all over his face. But if you hit someone where it leaves no marks, it remains between the two of you, which is a sign of respect, and the other guy will take it better.

(. . .)

<u>You must have a very strong will to live to have survived here so long.</u>

You have to have a bit of bad blood too. To make it out of all this shit around you, there's always the possibility of killing yourself. On those sleepless nights, you say to yourself, "I'll kill myself, and then all this bullshit goes away." Sometimes you have to weigh things, and find something to outweigh the desire to die. In my case the counterweight was always hatred: I always thought that the day I killed myself the doctors would celebrate, saying, "Finally we got that son of a bitch to kill himself." I'd hate to give them that pleasure, that victory.

(. . .)

In the last few years in Unit 20 I found myself on a

number of occasions standing by the wall grilling on the barbecue. There was a two-meter ladder right there and I could have easily climbed over the wall and escaped. I could have easily gotten away a couple of times. The other inmates used to tell me off for that: "You're an idiot, you should have taken your chance." I explained something very simple to them: I could have easily escaped. Got out of the Borda Hospital, made it into the streets. But even the Boy Scouts would have come looking for me. Escaping would mean being constantly on the run and with the likelihood of ending up in a shootout with someone. And I didn't want to end up like that. If that's how it goes, fine, maybe it'll be for other reasons, but not because I went looking for it.

(. . .)

Here I'm respected as an inmate who's lasted thirty-four years in prison and conducts himself properly. I have respect, I've earned my place through sheer force, and that's all fine.

But in here I'm still a murderer, and that's ultimately where my respect comes from. I could say, "Fine, this is the world I have to live in, I'm doing well here and I'm enjoying the fruits of my labors." But I think the essential problem is that I know there is much more out there, and I'm not ready to give up.

In your case, we can finish up our chat here and you'll leave, you can go into the city, and if you feel like having a beer you go to a corner store and you buy a beer. I've *forgotten* what beer tastes like. I've forgotten what many things taste like. You forget after so long.

Next to the prison, there's a little factory where they make nylon bags. Sometimes a truck comes to deliver materials. The smell of the truck, that smell of burnt petrol, the smell coming from the tailpipe is so strong. You can only smell it when the truck comes. Perhaps on the outside, you wouldn't even notice it. But it's not a smell that exists inside here, it's something you smell only every once in a while, so you notice it.

<u>What do you imagine it would be like, to be out of jail?</u>

When I think of freedom, of getting out . . . I don't want to be president, I don't want a car, I don't want to buy a house. My dream is to move to the country, to drink yerba maté under a shady tree, to seek out nature, seek out distance. There's no distance here. One of the problems is you become so used to short distances that long distances make you dizzy. When I was in Unit 20, sometimes at night I'd manage to sneak out to a little patio so I could look at the stars. And the stars made me dizzy. The farthest I can gaze is to that wall. I'm not used to anything bigger.

Another dream about the outside is going to a supermarket to see all the strange things they have now that I wouldn't be able to recognize. All the fruits and vegetables. You're speaking here to a guy who for thirty years has eaten potatoes, carrots, onions, and cabbage. The last time they ran tests on me, they had a sheet with little pictures and underneath I had to put their names. There was one picture I couldn't name. I said, "Shit, what the hell is that?" And the woman testing me said, "Don't you know what this is?" I told her it looked like a vegetable, but I didn't know which one. "It's broccoli," she said. "It's delicious—how could you not recognize it?" So I told her, "Ma'am, I've been in jail for thirty years, where do you think I would have seen a *broccoli*?" Same goes for a plum, or a peach.

The only expectation I have, the only transcendental debt, is to become a person. I've been a cockroach. And then I was a monster. Now I'm a prisoner. I would like to be a person. I'd never hide who I was, but . . . I'd like to be a normal person. The more I can blend in among everyone else, the better.

That's the debt I owe myself, to be just like everyone else. Lost in the crowd.

Acknowledgments

I would like to thank the team from the Prism Program from the Ministry of Justice and Human Rights in the 1st Federal Penitentiary Complex in Ezeiza, particularly Jessica Muniello, Ana Silva, Aldana Hosni, Ana Izaguirre, and Pablo Vitalich, for their kind collaboration.

I would also like to thank Miguel Ángel Caminos, Hugo Marietán, Zulema Fernández, Mariana Gorosito, Rubén Soro, Bernardo Beccar Varela, and M.R.

And in a broader and more existential sense, I'd like to thank Carina González, without whose influence this (and many other things besides) would never have happened.

Buenos Aires
September 2016

Carlos Busqued was born in Presidencia Roque Sáenz Peña, Chaco, Argentina, in 1970 and lives in Buenos Aires. His first novel, *Under This Terrible Sun*, was a finalist for the 2008 Herralde Prize and later adapted for film (*El Otro Hermano*, Adrian Caetano, 2017). *Magnetized* is his second book.

Samuel Rutter is a writer and translator from Melbourne, Australia. His work has appeared in *Gulf Coast*, *The White Review*, *A Public Space*, *T Magazine*, and elsewhere. Awarded a PEN Translates Prize in 2014, he has translated authors including Matías Celedón, Sònia Hernández, and Selva Almada.